THE ARROGANCE
OF INFINITY

THE ARROGANCE OF INFINITY

Tales of Transition from the Industrial to Technology Age

MIKE PICKETT

gatekeeper press™

Tampa, Florida

The Arrogance of Infinity: Tales of Transition from the Industrial to Technology Age

Published by Gatekeeper Press
7853 Gunn Hwy, Suite 209
Tampa, FL 33626
www.GatekeeperPress.com

Cover photo courtesy of Steven Ahlgren
Book cover design by Tom Witkowski, 9circlesfiction.com

Library of Congress Control Number: 2023936511

ISBN (paperback): 9781662938900
eISBN: 9781662938917

This is a memoir, and I couldn't figure out how to not dedicate it to a lifetime of people.

The book is dedicated to my wife, Mary Beth, who reads more than almost anyone I know, but "doesn't care for the memoir genre," and hasn't read this one.

To Mom and Dad… Ruth and Dave… Cece, Tom, and Pete.

To the siblings: chell-rhonda-ringo-jenny-mike-missy-andi, to Jarrod, and so many incredible nieces, nephews, cousins, uncles, and aunts.

To the Burnetts, O'Keefes, Seissegers, and Murphys.

To Mike, Tom, Darcy, Lynn, Joe, and Mary Ellen.

To the people of Nativity, CDH, VIS, STA, and the West 7th gang.

To all of 'The Dogs,' RHS '79, the scorer's table at "The Chuck," the boys of Savant, and the LAFT.

To Timmy, Matthew, Jimmy, Louie and their gals, and everyone who ever visited "The Pond," especially Francis: the dog they named a Pope after… oh… and this book is dedicated to Pooks, and whomever is lucky enough to marry her.

CONTENTS

INTRODUCTION

As a kid, I went to 11 schools; 12, if you count Romper Room with Miss Betty. My six siblings and I lived in suburbia and small to mid-sized towns. We grew up in natural pastures and concrete cities in an age powered by oil and coal, iron and steel.

Somewhere in the middle of the 20th century, the powers began to shift toward a New Age. Tubes, transistors, and microchips kicked off a virtual migration to the most progressive era in the history of humanity... so far.

These 'Tales of Transition' are the recollections of a Midwestern kid who rubbed up against a wide variety of challenges and blessings during the cyber-makeover. In them, I attempt to blend historical context and perspective with some humor, philosophy, and common tragedy.

The tales share the experiences of a large, close-knit family, and how we endured challenges such as a house fire, the premature death of a parent, and financial ruin.

They also include brushes with celebrity and notoriety such as meeting Neil Armstrong in our front yard a few weeks after he walked on the moon, a personal 30-year feud with Cal Ripken, and three hours of vodka-lemonades with Arnold Palmer. Alex Trebek toasted our marriage, and there was the day my wife stole personal property of the Clintons' from the White House. Her cousin, Tom Burnett, was on Flight 93.

My arrogant hope is to connect the daily grind of everyday life to unique experience and hopeful purpose – to remind people that we always possess the power to triumph over adversity. I want the reader to feel nostalgia and empathy, and to close this book with a sense that it's never too late to seek – and find – new joys.

These are 'Tales' because recollection isn't always as accurate as one thinks. My inspirations come from fond and formidable memories, and from writers and thinkers ranging from Dr. Seuss to Dorothy Parker, Mark Twain to Virginia Woolf, Frederick Douglass, Marcus Aurelius, Gandhi, and Ogden Nash. It's a quasi-autobiography that's out of order.

We humans live with the arrogance of infinity in our hearts, behaving as if our places and things, processes, ideas, and conditions, were created by – and forever belong to us.

We plow through life collecting ripple-causing memories and egotistical frustrations over all that is finite – as if we are not. In the end, when our mortality is finally measured, it is with the elements of infinity: Love, Grace, and Forgiveness.

This is the Arrogance of Infinity – a collection of real-life Tales about the transition from the Industrial to Technology Age.

PART ONE

NOW ARRIVING

When I was a tow-headed kid with a crew cut who wore striped t-shirts and hockey tape around the tips of his tattered sneakers, there were several passenger trains routed through Minneapolis and St. Paul, Minnesota. Great Northern had its *Empire Builder*, Burlington the *Zephyr*, and North Western the *400*. Northern Pacific had the *North Coast Limited*, Rock Island the *Twin Star Rocket*, and The Chicago, Milwaukee, St. Paul & Pacific Railroad – known as the Milwaukee Road – had their flagship *Hiawatha*; these were the engines of the Industrial Age.

Meanwhile, on TV, Lawrence Welk, Dick Rodgers, and Florian Chmielewski (shim-a-less-key) were delighting viewers with static camera shots of folks dancing in circles to Slavic music played by a concertina and a saxophone.

North American settlers who still had ties to the land were taking their last romantic spins with polka dancers and passenger trains. Boeing's 707 was lifting people above and beyond as rock 'n roll was warning folks to keep the white patent leather "off o' their Blue Suede Shoes."

The new heights and sounds of jet planes and rock 'n roll were age spots on the hands of industrialists, and more pain in the hearts of the indigenous. The 1960s micro-age foreshadowed the coming tech revolution with sleek speed, new rhythms, and futuristic peeks at outer space on television. Between Slavic dances, the emerging media began to paint revealing color over episodes of black-and-white Wild West lore.

Historical context and emerging trends meant nothing to a little towhead. I stood in awe on the platform at the Milwaukee Road Depot in Minneapolis as my oldest sisters boarded a big steel coach with seats so huge you could sleep in them.

Taking the girls to the train was a family affair but, since there were nine of us, you had to cast lots for the privilege to watch them leave. They'd wave at us from their seats with excitement that was magnified by hair pulled back in white headbands that matched their gloves and the teeth of their ear-to-ear grins.

The aging, relatively tiny train station in Minneapolis may as well have been Grand Central or Penn Station to me, but it only had four platforms - Grand Central has 44. That meant nothing as well; the quixotic drone of a single locomotive beneath the tin-roof of the train shed canopy, rusted I-beams, and massive iron rivets was all I needed to be drawn into the geriatric allure of Industrial Aged nostalgia.

I knew my time to ride the big steel rails would come, and happily waved in response to my sisters' hands that kept flapping as the train began to chug toward a romantic, ten-hour roll through parts of cities and towns never seen by the girls; it would carry them over rivers and through the woods. To grandmother's house they'd go.

My only train ride had been with Jimmy Brinkhaus and Tommy Kobold on the Dan Patch Line of the Northfield, Minneapolis, & Southern Railway. We climbed into an empty box car for a couple hundred yards as the freighter crawled along

Bailiff Place in our Bloomington, Minnesota neighborhood at speeds that were 'safely' slow enough to be overtaken by six-year-olds in tattered sneakers. That was the only train I ever 'hopped'. Cautionary tales of a kid* who slipped and had his leg cut off convinced me to bide my time for a big cushy seat on *The Hiawatha*.

I had to wait til I was twelve, when I was deemed old enough to take the trek down to grandmother's house by myself. The sisters were nearly grown up by then, and curb-dropped me and my powder-blue Samsonite at the downtown terminal with instructions to wait for the proper announcement before climbing on board.

There were more stops by then, so mine would be a 14-hour trek. The recorded broadcast echoed through the building: "Now boarding, Jefferson Lines and Continental Trailways service to Northfield, Faribault, Owatonna..." that was my bus.

A bus... and not even a Greyhound.

The announcement continued, "...Dodge Center, Rochester, Stewartville, Spring Valley, Decorah, New Hampton (home of Sara Lee), Oelwein, Waterloo, Vinton (famous for popcorn), Cedar Rapids, Iowa City, Mt. Pleasant, Fort Madison, Keokuk (World's Largest Street Fair) ..."

There were some small towns in there, too. One of the last stops would mock me; Burlington was famous for railroads.

The bus trips down through Iowa, to Mom's family farm in western Illinois all blend into one memory. I imagine a dozen rides, but it was probably about four, and I admit to artistic license in recounting them.

In my memories, Jefferson Lines wasn't so bad, but there was no observation car with a 360 view of the amber waves, no refreshments in the diner, and no place to explore except that tiny, overused rest room in the back. I'd play a balance game in that stinky little box by standing in a sports-stance and counting to see how long I could last without touching the walls as the bus bounced along Highway 63, or some crumbling County Road. It was a game of skill and will, in that you never really wanted to touch anything in there.

Jefferson Lines curb-dropped me in Waterloo for continuing service via Continental Trailways. The new rig had the same little box in back, but I'd already set a world record at Bus Bathroom Balance and would strike up a conversation or read a book. I read a lot of books. It took a full day in a Soviet Gulag to get from Oelwein to Ft. Madison one time as I read Alexander Solzhenitsyn's *One Day in the Life of Ivan Denisovich*.

Sometimes, I'd just look around at the characters. I saw a cute girl my age one time, in Stewartville, but she got off the bus too soon for me to gather courage. It was only three hours to Iowa City. Despite my lack of courage, the bus rides were good to me, they got me to the farm.

One thing I liked about riding high was being almost eye-to-eye with truck drivers like my uncle Benton 'Jiggs' Burton. Mom once asked what I wanted to be when I grew up.

"A truck driver," I replied.

I had Jiggs in mind. He was a tough country boy who could drive and fix anything. He could shuffle cards faster than anyone on the planet and finesse a 40,000-pound truck with no power steering using big, industrial-age-spotted hands. He was part cowboy, part man of the world, as he drove herds of cattle across the plains to big cities and stockyards at Kansas City, Chicago, and South St. Paul in a snub-nosed hauler that could be tucked into a modern sleeper cab.

Years later, I'd bypass the steel rails and bus rides and re-trace Jiggs' path to Illinois in a modern truck that could be steered with a little finger. In 2001, I ran into his son, cousin Bill. I hadn't seen them in more than a decade; not since time turned ten buildings and two feed lots on the farm into more tillable acres that grew soybeans and corn rather than family and livestock.

Family reunions were semi-annual affairs at the farm where cousins renewed best friendships then dispersed to not be seen or heard.

We'd drive cars at 13, shoot squirrels with .22s, and each other with BB guns. We'd ride branches of mulberry trees like rocking horses above bedsheets that would harvest fruit by the pailful rather than the one-at-a-time plucks of gooseberries. We'd stay clear of the bulls, stampede the hogs, and skim low and quiet in ponds, like alligators, then pounce with rocks to thump bullfrogs that would expand dinner menus for us, and the feral cats.

After supper, at a dining room table that could seat about 50, games would be dealt, talks would include politics and religion. Iced desserts came from fresh cream and wild berries that were hand-cranked by big spotted hands and little would-be industrialists. No matter how or when I got there, it was always summer at the farm – in the way I remember.

In 2001, when there was little left but gravestones and memories, I was pleasantly surprised to learn from cousin Bill that Jiggs, the old truck-driving shuffler, was still with us, about 30 miles south, in a Mt. Sterling, Illinois nursing home.

The receiving nurse pointed down a hall cluttered with service carts and orange fiberglass chairs shaped like ice cream scoops, to a man who was now of a tiny world and draped in a wheelchair he couldn't drive.

Jiggs didn't know me from a deck of Hoyles and looked up with grumpy disgust for interrupting his habitual gaze. When I reintroduced myself, his eyes flashed like the bulbs of a Polaroid. The mood, and his eyes, then got soft and syrupy as I thanked him for great childhood memories and recounted quail hunts, Sorghum Festivals, and Old Settlers' Days at the town square bandshell.

When there was nothing left to say, I said "Welp..." and eased up out of the scoop-chair. His eyes just blinked this time, with a fading, bittersweet resignation. I sensed he knew that other than his two kids, he'd just seen the last visitor from the outside world. He knew the freak coincidence, or divine intervention, was but a final glance at days-gone-by in a country farmhouse full of kids, card games, banjos, and roars of laughter. The picture had fully developed and started to fade. The cards had no more hands to shuffle.

I felt good, like a visiting angel, for a split-second, then slinked like a reaper down the hall of the Senior Dying facility before slumping in my pickup to spend the next ten minutes in a weep I didn't fully understand. A few weeks later, Jiggs went to see the outside world, forever. His legacy isn't on the Internet.

Jets and Zooms replace train rides that once were the connections to rural families and farms. The horsepower of a leaf-hauling F-150 exceeds the force of a snub-nosed cattle rig. Thick, age-spotted hands of industrial strength pass on, as slim fingers finesse keypads of code.

Things aren't as I wish to remember they were. The future – as it always must be – is now arriving.

Writer's note: Through a Bloomington, MN nostalgia page on Facebook, I learned that the story about the kid who lost a leg to train hopping was not just a parental scare tactic. It was Ronnie Knutson who tragically gave a leg that saved many others. God bless you, Ronnie.

PART TWO

EXPEDITIONS

For a seven-year-old kid who'd spent 90 percent of his life in a forest or field, the sidewalks beneath the cavernous buildings of big-city Minneapolis were a wonder; especially when being dragged by a 70-year-old Word War I Vet who kept pace with pedestrian traffic through an excellent memory and the rapid clickety-clack of a white cane.

Gramps gave life lessons to his eight grandsons by occasionally taking one of us to work with him at the Minnesota State Highway Department, known - in the age of hurry-up acronyms - as MNDOT. His job, reserved for a disabled vet, was daily management of the donut vending machines on each of the Highway Building's eight floors.

I was stealing glances at my all-time favorite building, the art deco Foshay Tower; a Washington Monument look-alike that was the tallest structure between Chicago and the West Coast from 1929 to '72. That's when Investors Diversified Services came along and stole the title with their evil, glass-and-steel IDS Tower.

My first classroom experience occurred atop the Foshay two years earlier in the studios of KMSP-TV, alongside Miss Betty, on the "Do Be a Do-Bee" set of the children's television show,

Romper Room. Despite getting to drive the Milk Truck, I was unable to parlay the performance into child stardom.

Gramps busted my reflections of youth with each tug of the hand, "Gotta keep up," he'd say. "Get the drift? If ya don't, I'll snow ya in."

I needed to keep pace so we could catch the connecting bus that would take us across the Mighty Mississippi, through the sprawling campus of the University of Minnesota, past St. Mary's – the hospital of my birth – and on to the mysterious land of Government, Fairgrounds, Ice Castles, and Catholics – St. Paul, Minnesota.

When it was my turn to make the epic journey with Gramps, I'd sleep in his big leather recliner and rise at 4:30 a.m. at 3444 Colfax in South Minneapolis. Today, the Pullman-style apartment with a garage stall and location in trendy "Uptown," is priced like a New York City flat and a dream address for millennials. Gram would have the "most important" meal waiting but, with bakers in St. Paul filling a room with glazed and sprinkled and jellied pleasures, my interest in nutrition was thin.

Before any taste of the rare delights came the expedition. It was a half block up Colfax to 34th, then three blocks over to Lyndale where we'd fill the clinking coin counter of a green-and-white bus that would take us downtown to Hennepin Avenue.

Hennepin was aptly named for a Franciscan priest (as in – who else could forgive its existence?) and was one of two Skid Rows in Minneapolis that were populated by mostly white men whose post-war dreams and ambitions had been rediscovered in day-jobs, flop houses, panhandling, thievery, and booze.

We'd walk a few more blocks past Nicollet and Marquette to 2nd Avenue where we'd complete the transfer to an eastbound bus. I'd gape at more buildings along the way: another art-deco tower, The Rand; the gothic spires of Northwestern Bell Telephone; Farmers & Mechanics Bank – whose entrance was guarded by depression-era sculptures of lean and powerful-looking men; Northern States Power had mascot Reddy Kilowatt; and the top of the Northwestern National Bank building had a color-coded ball of glass that told the weather. By the age of nine, I knew Minneapolis architecture like most kids knew baseball cards.

After the bus transfer we'd pass one of the city's most significant buildings, one that housed the apex of media power and influence in the upper Midwest: The Minneapolis Star and Tribune Company, a business that relied on more than 10,000 independent distributors to circulate almost a million newspapers six days a week, and more than a million on Sundays. The distributors were 12-to-16-year-old kids who were also in charge of sales, revenue collection, and local inventory control.

St. Paul, however, had a building far more impressive than any in Minneapolis. The Cathedral of St. Paul is the fourth largest church in the U.S. and the largest outside of New York City and Washington, DC. It sits on the city's highest hill, and the massive, 120-foot wide, copper dome rises another 306 feet with such ominous presence as to never be taken for granted. The first time I saw it, I knew Minneapolis had more big business towers, but God's headquarters was across the river.

We couldn't see the cathedral for most of the seven-mile trip of starts-and-stops along University Avenue – the main drag between the cities. The route was a gorge of two, and three-story structures that had aged through a century of major world conflict and the Great Depression. The buildings that had been torn down were paved with asphalt and loaded with New/Used automobiles for sale at the best prices, but probably not the best values, in town.

The Highway Building was perched alongside its brand-new Interstate 94 that was near completion, but traffic-free in the summer of '68 as a river of concrete cured in anticipation of joining America's most recent innovation in distribution: the Eisenhower National System of Interstate and Defense Highways. The folks in the building – Gramps' customers – engineered the ramming of I-94 through the "Rondo Neighborhood," just as their counterparts in New York, Philadelphia, Indianapolis, Nashville, Tulsa, et al, had done to the burgeoning centers of Black culture throughout the nation.

Half of Gramps' customers looked up at the cathedral, and half across expansive lawns to the gleaming white marble of our state's capitol – a building that in 1968 represented, to me, the hope of humanity, but 50 years later would come to epitomize waste and corruption.

The green-and-white bus, that looked like it belonged in every American city, took a turn off University Avenue and stopped a half block from our destination. Once inside the Highway Building's commissary, I'd marvel at Gramps' sense of feel for the right keys that opened access to his daily process. He had a broom closet of an office that had a couple of bus carts, general supplies, and a cast iron safe with a big dial that was just as cool as they looked on TV.

Work would begin with packaging freshly baked doughnuts, eclairs, and Bismarcks, which are jelly doughnuts from Germany where they were called 'Berliners' before being renamed after Chancellor Otto Von Bismarck. In the U.S., the original name stuck in heavily concentrated German populations and led to the localized joke that John F. Kennedy's "Ich bin Ein Berliner" speech translated to "I am a jelly doughnut."

My job was to slide pastries into cellophane bags, fold them over, then swipe the package over a stainless-steel hot plate to create a quick-melt seal. Back in the '60s, adults believed the pain of error was the fastest way to teach.

We'd visit vending machines on each of eight floors – using modern, operator-free elevators with push buttons the whole time – to swap out day-olds for fresh doughnuts and pour square metal buckets of coins into canvas cash bags. Some of the day-olds would be sold to frugal palates at half-price, some would go to churches, most of the leftovers went to custodial pals of Gramps who carried obvious indications of their military service.

It wasn't rare in those days to see Buffalo nickels, last minted in 1938, and Mercury dimes from 1916-45, in circulation. Once in a while, we'd even come across Indianhead pennies that were minted from 1859-1909. The 'Wheatback' pennies had only been out of circulation for a decade, so Gramps put those collectibles aside in a WWII surplus shell box to save for future generations.

The blind man's sense of feel would again come into play back at his office where he'd sift coins through his fingers. His keen sense could feel the difference between the more valuable discontinued coins and the new mints of Washington, Jefferson, Abe, and FDR.

He'd let the modern coins fall away, then buy out - at face value - the more valuable stock for his side venture as a coin broker. We'd swing back to the 3rd and 7th floors to visit Gramps' coin-collector buddies who would purchase the currency at wholesale, then turn it again at pawn and coin shops. The gratuitous insider trading was forgiven in lieu of their Nine-to-Five fates as cattle in 40x100 foot rooms with no dividers, just dozens of perfectly aligned rows of metal desks separated by the exact amount of space it takes to get a mail or doughnut cart down the aisle.

The day would come full circle with a return trip to Minneapolis on the green and white bus where we would be dropped at the doorstep of Ballantine VFW Post #246 on Lyndale and Lake Street. Gramps would set me up at the bar with a soda and instructions to keep an eye out for Gram while he conducted business – a card game – in the club room. Gram would show within an hour in a shiny Buick Skylark from her job as a bookkeeper at the world's largest retailer, Sears & Roebuck Company, before driving us weary workers back home.

My Pop's folks exuded an air of wealth; everything was always so tidy and neat at 3444 Colfax – from the kitchen to their clothes, to the air-conditioned Skylark. Unlike mom's home on the farm, where bugs, dust, and animals were first-cousins, Rex and Beulah's apartment was air-tight with order and cleanliness. It was many years before I came to recognize the origins of their elegant efficiency.

There was no financial wealth for my grandparents; merely self-preserving self-discipline born out of a love of freedom. They grew up in a world dominated by monarchs, sultans, emperors, and kaisers. A hundred years ago, the only nations free from totalitarians were the United States, France and – if you want to count a micro-nation with Captains Regents as heads of state – San Marino.

The 'Centennials' of the early 1900s were nostril-deep in real-life, Occupy-the-World battles to determine whether people would live in Individual Liberty or be lorded over by tyrannies of the extreme right and left. 'One-percenters' of the early 20th century owned more than most of the world's wealth – they owned most of the world's people. And when they weren't happy with another totalitarian, or if they were feeling a need for a bit more power, they'd send millions of youthful male subjects to go fight for it.

During one of those fights, on September 13, 1918, at the battle of St. Mihiel, France, Corporal Rex Levering Pickett of the American Expeditionary Force, was riddled with shrapnel and lost his sight to Kaiser Wilhelm's artillery and mustard gas. It led to two lifetimes of stoic organization that was my grandparents' response to the human inequity that has existed since the dawn of time.

It led to a job at the Highway Building for a 70-year-old blind man who parlayed the opportunity into life lessons for his grandchildren.

***

Part Two has an addendum that features my favorite story about our Grandfather, Rex Levering Pickett Sr. It was delivered as the "Faith Minute" at the Nativity Church Men's Club meeting in St. Paul, Minnesota on Veteran's Day, November 11, 2021.

"The Faith Minute is a brief reminder of why we gather… tonight we gather on Veteran's Day.

My grandfather was a devout man – with an edge – one of those guys with an unshakable demeanor who was perpetually positive. The traits came to him easily, and the hard way. He got a free trip to Europe when he was 20... and won six thousand bucks playing craps in Paris. He sent three grand home to his mom, then took a buddy to the south of France for a 28-day tour.

It was very specifically a 28-day holiday... because 30 would be desertion... they were AWOL from the United States Army. This was September 1, 1918 – back when three grand could buy a house and a car, and deserters could get shot.

Gramp's rank got busted from "the guy who aims the artillery," to "the forward guy who spots targets." Less than two weeks later, he lay on the battlefield at St. Mihiel, France for two days with a body full of shrapnel and eyes blinded by mustard gas.

My blind grandfather worshipped with thanks every Sunday. He spent his last years hauling grandsons to work with him on a 12-mile city bus expedition from south Minneapolis to the Highway Building in St. Paul where he filled donut vending machines and taught us perpetually positive life lessons. He wasn't one in a million, he was one in millions who have been unshakably devoted to faith and freedom.

Archbishop Broglio of the US Military Archdiocese said, "The privilege to hold differing opinions and faiths, and express them openly, is the direct result of the sacrifices of our veterans."

Let's be extra thankful for our Veterans today… and renew our devotion to God, who endows all our rights and freedoms – sometimes, with an edge.

Pro Liberis (for the children)."

PART THREE

SEARCHING FOR NORMAL

The year 1968 was anything but typical. For the first time ever, humans transplanted a heart and circled the moon. A pandemic – the H3N2 "Hong Kong" flu – took millions in confirmation of globalism. Fifty-five days separated the assassinations of our nation's Reverend, Dr. Martin Luther King Jr., and his friend and presidential candidate, Robert F. Kennedy.

Thousands more Americans died during the Viet Cong's Tet Offensive, then – three months later – U.S. soldiers massacred 500 Vietnamese villagers at My Lai. The Soviets invaded Czechoslovakia for wanting to be free, North Koreans seized the USS Pueblo for trying to peek through the keyhole of their regime, and the British had their first successful invasion of the USA using Stones, Beatles, Yardbirds, and Hermits.

In 1968, social reformists protested the Democrats at their convention in Chicago, Smith and Carlos raised Black Panther fists at the Mexico City Olympics, a bank in Philadelphia hired a machine named ATM to replace a teller, the first Big Mac cost forty-nine cents, and the maiden voyage of the 747 LuxuryLiner went airborne with a piano bar.

Our family lived on Normal Street. No euphemism intended.

We lived at 108 North Normal in Macomb, a small city – or big town – of about 20,000 that is home to Western Illinois University. Our house was three blocks from the campus where Pop accepted a job as director of food services so we could move closer to Mom's family.

I was in first grade and my lifestyle outside of school amounted to little more than playing with trucks and exploring so - no matter where we lived - life was probably gonna be normal. But this was a time of seminal change for the USA, the world, and especially for me.

My best friend back in Bloomington, Jimmy Brinkhaus, was a head taller than me. We pounded around together, built forts, climbed trees, ate wild rhubarb, and even hopped a train. In Illinois, he was replaced by a little girl named "Ginger."

Jennifer "Ginger" Hopkins lived across the normal street and even though I have sisters just months in either direction, Ginger picked me as a pal. She and I met in the middle at play as we dug roads and fashioned castles in the dirt to create fairytale empires for her village of Trolls and Little Kiddles dolls.

We sneaked into the college gymnasium – with access and inspiration from my resourceful brother – to fearlessly jump from folded bleachers onto the big, white, competition trampolines that would pogo-bounce us high in the air to land on padded mats that were almost as thick as we were tall.

We'd drive like grownups without accident in an abandoned car in the alley behind her house. We waved sparklers, threw firecrackers, and lit charcoal snakes on the 4th of July with only minor incident.

There were long treks on bikes past the house full of hippies to ride up, down, and around a newly paved parking lot at the Methodist Church four blocks away. We explored the mysterious woods on campus to discover an ancient, moss-covered amphitheater that nobody else in the world knew about.

We ate lots of peanut butter and jelly.

It was two blocks to Dairy Queen for a nickel cone after I helped my brother with his paper route, or when she found a returnable soda bottle, or one of us lost a tooth. We saved a jackrabbit from injury and nurtured him in a makeshift cage that was sturdy enough to hold in a wounded bunny, but not strong enough to hold out a prowling tomcat. Then we mourned together.

We lived and learned on a Normal Street, in an atypical age.

Ginger's parents were groovy professors who went by uncomfortable names – George and Elaine – in place of the Mr. and Mrs. They sent her to a private school, so she wasn't at Woodrow Wilson Elementary to stop me from stealing Stanley Beacraft's eraser, or to save me from Mrs. Stickle (Wickle-Popsicle) and the well-earned punishment of a whack on the hands with a rubber-tipped map pointer and time in a corner wearing a dunce cap.

We lived an ordinary moment when a little black-and-white Admiral TV was replaced with an 18" Zenith that showed both channels – including the NBC Peacock – in living color. It was normal for us to envy 'rich' families who could afford battery operated toys as well as the batteries that were not included.

Our first rides on a school bus took us way across town to a huge gymnasium where we'd line up to be inoculated against smallpox, the measles, and polio. On automobile rides – when grownups were driving – Ginger and I would see littered curbs and ditches.

Throwing garbage out car windows wasn't normal, but it wasn't illegal yet either, and once a car or farm implement reached a point beyond the healing magic of bailing wire, it became part of the environment – as an amusement, a gigantic planter, or new habitat for wildlife. In 1968, rusted roadside iron, and trash, was as common as the scar from the needles of a smallpox shot.

In that year, it was uncommon for differing cultures to interact on a regular basis. The lessons to "love one another as oneself" had been delivered for centuries, but it still didn't feel normal. The love lacked a sincere sense of trust, safety, and plausibility. We separately coexisted, with and without scars.

The simple, fearless exploration of the Normal neighborhood in an atypical year couldn't last. Ginger eventually went off to Chicago to become grown-up Jennifer. I left too, maintaining my juvenile penchant for selfish exploration and discovery.

We found new towns, new best friends, and stayed steady on a quest for new normal. It led to a remarkable marriage for me, a new home, and new friends who became family and reintroduced fearlessness and new fears in a neighborhood where our daughter could begin her own explorations.

2020, like 1968, was anything but typical. I don't know where my first love, Ginger is, but I know Jimmy Brinkhaus is still taller. And I know we can't change the challenge of grown-up life by pretending, or through what-if dreams of a fairytale empire. I do know I can reflect and rekindle a childhood spirit to help bring context to a typical age of atypical events. I can conjure a day when 'normal' meant the joy of innocent hope and the courage summoned by natural challenge.

The Normal house in Macomb is gone – replaced by another ATM. The USA is trade partners with Vietnam, and the Soviet Union no longer exists. There's also a new worldwide pandemic, and the North Korean government is still dictated by a man named Kim. Technology and medical innovations continue to surge in geometric progression as protests magnify the intrinsic inequity of humanity.

There's no going back to Normal; it only exists as a thoroughfare of memories, and a side-road of hope where a dream can drive.

PART FOUR

RACE & RUST

You didn't have to look very closely to see the whittle marks on my third-grade Pinewood Derby car. I crafted the racer with a pocketknife that Grandad Aleshire taught me to use so I could make a frog gig or makeshift bow and arrow. The finished product had clumps of aqua and orange Testor's paint on the chassis and gobs of glue in the nail axles. It ended up being a miracle car.

It was 1970 and we had moved to Lima, Ohio, (Lima as in bean, not Lima as in Peru) after Pop received an offer he couldn't refuse, a position as regional consultant for International Multifoods and their chain of Sweden House Smorgasbord restaurants. Lima was one in hundreds of aging industrial hubs at the time. The mid-sized cities were distributors of steel and oil that had consumed, replaced, and modernized the nation's network of small towns that once served independent growers of grain and livestock. The small towns had consumed, replaced, and modernized the tribal networks of hunters and gatherers who blazed the trails that would become roads of automated industry.

Our year in the Buckeye State, spring of '69 to summer of '70 was an interesting time – for us, the state of Ohio, and for a nation that had launched races against each other, space, and time.

The first man on the moon, Neil Armstrong, was from Wapakoneta, Ohio, 20 miles south of Lima. We went to his homecoming parade and drank a local cream soda called Wapakoneta Moon Sauce. A couple weeks later – as my brother, Ringo, and I were in the front yard tossing Styrofoam airplanes powered by rubber bands and plastic propellers – our neighbor waved us over.

"Boys, come on over here," she said. "I want you to meet an old friend of mine." We obeyed, then stood paralyzed after shaking the hand that was first to touch the moon. The man seemed almost embarrassed by our amazement; he offered a humble grin, and said, "nice to meet you, boys."

My brother and I didn't celebrate and hug, and giggle about the rare honor – as we had when we met Farsell MacBee of the Minnesota Vikings – meeting Neil Armstrong in your front yard in 1969 was like having tea with Churchill in '45, or lunch with Lindbergh when he returned from Paris in '27 – we just stared at each other in disbelief.

The meeting kicked off a series of uniquely historic events in Ohio that year: the Cuyahoga River in Cleveland infamously caught fire in ultimate confirmation that the 'industry' in 'Industrial' had gotten way out of hand. An unusual amount of snow that winter made us Minnesotans feel right at home and we were inspired to break out Pop's golf clubs for a pickup street hockey game. Things really got busy in the spring of '70 with the drama of Apollo 13 and the National Guard killing of four students at Kent State near Akron. 17-year cicadas emerged from the ground like millions of tiny zombies to lay an apocalyptic blanket of insects over every inch of ground, and then, of course, there was the Pinewood Derby at Shawnee Elementary School.

Lima was at peak population of 53,000 at the time, and a prototype of smoke-belching boomtowns from Allentown, Pennsylvania, to Gary, Indiana, and Superior, Wisconsin that turned raw ore from mines in Minnesota, Wisconsin, Michigan, and Alabama into the iron and steel that was needed to defeat the dictators who believed in master races and kept trying to take over the world in the 20th Century.

By the late '60s, oxidizing iron in the region known as the 'Rust Belt' was disintegrating like a time-bomb fuse. We drove through Pittsburgh, 'Steel City,' that year. I can't recall the skyline because it was hidden by a cloud of carbon and sulfur that looked thick enough to pack like a charcoal gray snowball.

Within a decade, billions and billions of infrastructure dollars would run out on Rust Belt cities to take up with investment bankers and leave behind jobless families to scratch their heads, and the soot off their walls, as they searched for places to compete in the workforce.

Lima lost its Locomotive Works, then its railroads. The nation's largest manufacturer of school buses, Superior Coach, wasn't there for the kids. Clark Machines, Airfoil Textron, and Westinghouse Electric Corporation employed no one. Lima was left with an Army Tank Plant and a Standard Oil refinery and the population shrank to 35,000 embattled, and well-oiled souls.

My Pinewood Derby entry wobbled down the track in 1970, beside two sleek racers. We all were ahead of another kid who needed a grandpa who could whittle. His dad, like mine, must have been a week-long traveler. A typical week had Pop on the road from Ashtabula to Zanesville. It wasn't as though he didn't care if I won a six-inch plastic trophy, but with nine mouths to feed, he was on a different track.

My older brother, Ringo, was an over-achieving member of the Webelos and could've helped me craft the car – if he hadn't been busy building natural playgrounds in the woods near the Ottawa River. He'd hack paths through thick brush, pick a spot with a decent clearing, then slash large liana vines that hung from the trees so we could swing through the forest like Tarzan.

We built a two-by-three-foot Hoover Dam look-alike with working spillways in a clay drainage ditch, then staged a World War II battle reenactment with our plastic army men. Our ordnance was firecrackers, and one cherry bomb that took out the Germans, and the dam before they could flood the surrounding field - before Mom could throw us in the stockade for insubordination. We were nine and twelve years old, and my brother was the greatest engineer in the world.

The Ottawa River was a couple hundred yards from our house, and like most 'Rust Belt' waterways, it had issues; 77,000 gallons worth. In 1970, an oil pipeline burst and spilled into the city water supply to give the river the appearance of a free-flowing alley puddle. We couldn't figure out how mom knew we were playing in the river – which was expressly forbidden. I guess she intuitively knew Mr. Rockefeller hadn't hired us down at the refinery.

I was living in my 5th home, Ringo his 7th, and we had no complaints. We had experienced the great suburban boom in Bloomington, Minnesota with rural fields not far from construction sites that offered ready access to building materials for go-carts and tree forts; we had lived in an Illinois college town that demonstrated equally the lifestyles of progressive Hippies and throwback farmers. Our childhood journeys were a race from place to place, and we always had mom's childhood home, the Aleshire Farm, as a touchstone.

In Lima, we lived on Riverview Drive in Ottawa Hills. It was a flat street that met the river in a dead end. Our neighbors were more upscale than we were accustomed to; the kids of dentists and attorneys were friends but didn't share our sense of adventure. Ringo's intuition, and my evolving ability to keep up, led us across Highway 117 to Seriff Road a half-mile away, where we met the Wright brothers. No relation to the famous flyers of Akron; these Wrights were Black kids who shared a love of tackle football and welcomed a couple more players.

Our short time in Ohio didn't create long-lasting bonds, but John Wright became the closest thing I had to a best friend. Mrs. Wright served us pot roast at their home one night and didn't make me eat the cooked carrots. This was a dereliction of her duties. In those days, there was an understanding that parents would treat visiting kids as one of their own. But she didn't, and I was thankful. After supper, she brought popcorn for the pile of kids on a sofa to eat, then stood over us as we watched Gunsmoke and the Flip Wilson Show on a 16-inch black-and-white screen.

I imagine her thoughts to be of hope as she looked at young people who were still too naïve to know the biases, frustrations, and resentment that can permeate interactions between human races. All John Wright and I knew was that together, we dominated third-grade recess football games.

To me, fifty plus years later, the raw emotions and desperate violence of the early '70s still feels much more valid – and justified – than our 21st century 'wokeness' that seems to be on a redundant, ineffective crusade of blame that targets an indefinable 'Man' and makes sacred our systemic bureaucracies.

In 1970 we were only a couple years removed from the assassinations of Dr. Martin Luther King and Bobby Kennedy, and less than a decade beyond John Kennedy's death. The wounds and strides of civil rights battles were fresh and ongoing. A month after we moved from Ohio back to Minnesota, racial tensions and guns flared in Lima. Christine Rick, a woman about the same age as Mrs. Wright, lay dead not far from the house on Seriff Road where I was treated to pot roast, no carrots, and popcorn.

"Negro is Killed by Police," the headline said…

Ten days later and 150 miles west, sleek Soap Box Derby cars were racing down the hills of Akron, Ohio. It was the last year girls were excluded from the competition. Long gone were the crates of wood and old tractor seats strapped on two-by-four frames with bailing wire and half-bent nails. The cars had taken on the aerodynamic looks of miniature Indy cars. Seventeen years earlier, the Akron race had inspired an indoor version of the gravity competition that led to my whittling a seven-inch block of pine down to five miraculous ounces of wood, clumps, and gobs.

Despite dramatic design advances, Pinewood and Soapbox Derby winners of 1970 could still be perceived with a human sense, the naked eye. Our neighborhoods were the same. Separation was easy to see. Today, division is more prominent than ever, but the lines aren't as clear. We try to measure our races with integrated technology and every human sense – except maybe, love – as politics and self-interest drive us, like downhill blocks of wood on wheels.

We modern humans hasten toward automatic equity and virtual ease, as we abandon real wisdom and camaraderie. During the last gasp of the Industrial Age, we awoke from our ecological ignorance and gave up on smokestacks that billowed plumes of carbon and sulfur into the air. We shut off culverts that pumped toxic chemical sewage into rivers and lakes. The ages taught us to make a stone wheel, how to conquer fire, and split the atom a billion times. We developed Artificial Intelligence that can measure, analyze, and judge every thought... but we can't seem to master the simple math of division.

In 1903, Orville Wright of Dayton, Ohio took the first airplane flight for humanity with great expectation. Not long after World War II, he said:

> *"We dared to hope we had invented something that would bring lasting peace to the earth... we were wrong ... (but) I feel about the airplane much the same as I do in regard to fire. That is, I regret all the terrible damage caused by fire, but I think it is good for the human race..."*

The kit for a Pinewood car is pretty much the same as it's always been, but the Derby is not exempt from homogenized technology. Cub Scout packs gather in state-of-the-art woodshops with laser beams, wind tunnels, and coefficient measuring devices rather than on a back porch, or in a garage with a pile of tools. These days, if a kid's parent is off in Zanesville, he/she can just pull up a YouTube and crank out a competitive rig from one of several pre-approved templates.

The independents are still out there, though. Their cars launch from systemic starters then wobble down composite tracks to be measured and judged, so everyone knows who they are. The Buckeye kids at the Shawnee Pinewood Derby in 1970 witnessed my independent miracle car... it didn't finish last.

We accumulate clumps and gobs of life as we wobble toward an unknown finish line. We choose between tracks of consoling forgiveness or corrosive hate, and we don't have to look very closely to see the whittle marks on the soul of a nation in transition.

When we pause and reflect and look closely, we see – it's not about the race – it's about the journey.

PART FIVE

ICE AND FIRE

On Palm Sunday Eve of 1971, mom drove toward home on a dark stretch of road in eastern Iowa that had scant lane markings and even less directional signage. U.S. Highway 218 was typical of the narrow paths of crumbling asphalt that was the rural trunk highway system of the day. The Minnesota North Stars were playing the Philadelphia Flyers in the regular season finale, and mom was messing with the AM radio dial in a futile attempt to keep announcer Al Shaver tuned in - just in case Ted Harris would get into a scrap. Shaver called hockey fights like it was Ali vs. Frazier.

The '68 Ford Falcon station wagon was loaded with kids, but no seat belts, and bounced up and down the hills at speeds beyond posted limits as it grabbed the road's uneven edges that jerked the car to, and fro, and whoa! Three of us sat in back, clenching the front seat with fears that mom was falling asleep and we'd all soon be plunging into the deep dark woods. Sister Jenny up front finally asked mom if she was OK and could she please slow down or stop for a while.

"What!?" Mom blew off our concern. "Oh, honey... I'm not falling asleep. I thought you were all listening to the game. We're fine!"

Not much later, an Iowa trooper would provide the pause Jenny had requested. After pulling over, mom put the paralyzing fear of God into each of us with a point of her finger and an unmistakable command: "Not a God-damned word," she said.

The Trooper was polite, but stern. "License and registration, please, ma'am."

"I don't have a license, officer. My house just burned."

He went compassionate. "Oh, my. I'm sorry to hear that ma'am. What brings you to Iowa?"

"I'm taking the kids to my parents' in Illinois. We don't know what we're going to do."

"I understand," the Trooper nodded. "Would you please slow it down. We don't need another tragedy on our hands."

"Yes, officer. I certainly will."

The Trooper flashed his light through the car at faces that were still petrified by mom's directive. We must have looked like a modern-day version of the Joads. "Uh, well, God Bless you folks," he said to mom with a mixed look of admiration and pity.

After he left, Jenny said, "Mom, your license didn't burn in the fire." Her license expired in 1961 but Mom never bothered to renew.

"I didn't lie, honey. I told him I don't have a license."

Three weeks earlier, Mother Nature had sent an Advance Team to Burnsville to see if it was ready for Spring, but the State's high school hockey tournament was approaching, and the boys were still playing boot hockey on soggy rinks and driveways. Our playground squads would assume names of traditional hockey powers like the Broncos of International Falls, the Governors of St. Paul Johnson, the Minneapolis Southwest Indians, or the small but mighty Roseau Rams whose school of

350 kids brought a disproportionate amount of hockey talent down from the Canadian border almost every year.

Neighborhood buddy Duke Boeser's dad, Lyle, had called Pop to see if I could skip school with the Boeser boys to watch one of the nation's premiere prep tournaments on TV. Pop had played in the '48 tourney for St. Louis Park and was fully in favor of the truancy. On 'Tourney Thursday' we'd play more hockey on our knees in carpeted hallways with cut-off hockey sticks and puck-balls made of toilet paper wrapped in black hockey tape. Many of us haven't gone to school or worked on Tourney Thursday ever since.

On Tuesday the 9th, as Duke and I sat in a fourth-grade classroom at Edward D. Neill Elementary, our heads spun to the window - as if catching a glimpse at a speeding fire truck would give us insight into the emergency-in-progress.

"I'd laugh if that was my house," I said with a cynical crack.

Duke shook his head with a 'shame on you' look. "Don't even say that," he said.

Within 24 hours, my brother, five sisters and I were picking through clothing the neighborhood had hurriedly gathered at the school gymnasium, so we'd have something to wear.

I didn't laugh about the house fire, but never cried, either. Our parents were steadfast in keeping our lives as functional as possible. They made it seem as if a house burning was part of the natural order, like crashing on your bike, or getting caught out in the rain. You get up and lick your wounds, you change your clothes, you scramble for food and shelter. That's life.

By Saturday, the Edina Hornets had won their 2nd state championship in three years and were on their way to becoming the most envied high school in the state of Minnesota. I don't recall who won the carpet battles of Boeser's basement.

The family scattered for a few weeks, a few stayed with our faux cousins, the McChesneys, with whom we once shared back yards in Bloomington cul-de-sacs, and we spent some time in rooms at the Fair Oaks Motor Hotel in Minneapolis – a property owned by family friend, W. R. Frank. On April 3rd, that day before Palm Sunday, while mom took four of us to Illinois, the three oldest kids remained behind to help Pop with the family's four restaurants that our parents had purchased from International Multifoods.

On a larger stage, Richard Nixon was president and still very popular at the time. His Environmental Protection Agency (EPA) was a few months old, and he was pursuing "Peace with Honor" to end the bloody Cold War quagmire in a place called Vietnam – or 'French IndoChina' by the colonizers who were being kicked out of southeast Asia. In '71 Nixon prepared for "The Week that Changed the World," an historic trip to see China's communist dictator, Mao Tse Tung, and open the gates of trade. Mao had closed China to the world in 1949, but the Commie knew a good thing when he saw it. The impact of the presidential visit continues to redefine the World Order some 50 years later.

As one of the fastest and most accurate typists in the DC steno pool in the early '50s, mom typed for then Vice President Nixon and former First Lady Eleanor Roosevelt. I still have the autographed lithograph of the Capitol building he gave to Mom as a thank you gift. It's smoke-stained and still has a faint smell of smoldered ruins.

By August of 1974, Mr. Nixon would leave the White House for lying and covering up an operation that spied on his opponents at the Watergate hotel. The scandal, and disgraceful resignation of a president who was as strategically savvy as any in our history, shook confidence in the good ol' USA to its core.

Japanese manufacturers were beginning to make automobiles that were superior to those coming out of our Motor City, and riots in Ohio, Mississippi, New York, New Jersey, and Massachusetts combined with public disgust over Vietnam to plant seeds of doubt and self-loathing along with the perception that the 'World's Melting Pot' couldn't boil the nation's rotten eggs of corruption and bigotry.

Despite the tumultuous times, life went on with a sense of normalcy in many homes. Ours wasn't one of them.

We made it safely to Illinois, but back home, the Cruelest Month had more ill winds for Pop. He was the only one in the house as it burned and had managed to escape by jumping off the second-floor deck into the snow with shaving cream on his face, one suit and a box of birth certificates in his arms. A construction worker from the half-built house behind ours ran up to Pop and said, "Hey mister, your house is on fire!"

As Pop plodded barefoot through the snow in a robe, he said, "No shit, Sherlock."

Days later, he had borrowed Grams' Buick while my sister Chell drove his Ford to and from the restaurants. A thief broke into the Buick and stole his suit while, almost simultaneously, Chell was in an accident that totaled the Ford.

Needless to say, by Mom's birthday on April 17th, the complications of lodging and transportation could have put a damper on the day. She shared the date with close family friend, Dorothy Graw, one-time *Queen for a Day* in Australia, and one of several female friends of powerful personality who augmented my upbringing in an atmosphere where women were anchors and icons.

The personalities persisted through the complications at their birthday celebration that year. Mom, Dorothy and their iced-tea klatch, like Nixon, extended an olive branch to a communist by toasting Soviet Premier Nikita Khrushchev, whose birthday was the day before. Unlike Nixon's initiative, their toast would be tongue-in-cheek and conclude with, "the miserable bastard" followed by howls of laughter that were synonymous with gatherings of Mom and her friends.

The weather fluctuated from freezing to balmy in April that year as my cronies and I played on. We weren't ready to put away the hockey sticks. The North Stars had upset the St. Louis Blues in the first round of the NHL playoffs and would face hockey's most legendary team – the Montreal Canadiens, or 'Les Habitants' to French Canadians.

For our band of buddies who would eventually be known as 'The Dogs,' this would extend hockey season a couple more weeks until 'The Habs' bumped the Stars in game six on April 29th. We'd accept the late arrival of Spring, drop the sticks and gloves, and pick up the bats and balls to embrace another of life's cycles.

On the AM radio dial, the top song in March of '71 was "One Bad Apple" by Michael and the Jackson Five. This gave way to "Just my Imagination," by the Temptations, and Three Dog Night's, "Joy to the World" – all the boys and girls – before Don McLean's epic song and poem, "American Pie", would take the top spot later that year.

For the Rex and Patricia Pickett household, 1971 would be the year the music, but not the spirit, would die. From March 9th forward, my parents would be consumed by a half decade of daily battles against forces of life that would include a judicial battle over the house fire, economic uncertainty that caused people to stop spending $3.95 for all-you-can-eat meals at our restaurants, and – not the least of which – a cancer diagnosis in Mom.

Our parents, with help from the oldest girls, shielded the youngest of us from the constant uncertainty. Laughter and joy was often self-deprecating, but always present. I doubt they had much time to contemplate those whose lives were more challenging than ours, but based on the philosophies they ingrained in us, I know they were aware.

They continued to teach compassion and demonstrate contempt for bigotry. If mom heard one of us parrot the overt prejudices of the day, she'd issue a "fear of God" warning like the one she gave in the Ford Falcon. She'd remind us that not only were condescending thoughts toward others philosophically wrong, in our household, they may be hazardous to one's physical health.

As she took us on that Easter pilgrimage to the farm, the entire nation was driving Chevys to their Levies in attempts to re-imagine the good times of the once just and righteous nation that re-financed the globe after World War II.

Pop was tougher than most, but he would agree that mom was the glue. During the trials of the early '70s, he had to be hospitalized for exhaustion – quite a feat for a Naval Academy Marine. As Mom fought cancer, she guarded the fort, rallied the troops, and ran the business until his return.

The Joads in the movie version of Steinbeck's *The Grapes of Wrath* come to mind again when I think of my parents and those years. The final scene summarizes the lives of millions of people who miraculously endured an era of far greater and more widespread challenge: the Dust Bowl and Great Depression.

In the scene, Pa tells Ma how she was the one who kept the family together during the toughest times, and says, "*...we shore takin' a beatin', Ma.*"

Ma chuckles. *"I know. Maybe that makes us tough. Rich fellas come up an' they die, an' their kids ain't no good, an' they die out. But we keep a-comin'. We're the people that live. Can't nobody wipe us out. Can't nobody lick us. We'll go on forever, Pa. We're the people."*

Hockey tournaments will be played each year, the ice will melt and flow into the following season. New songs, genres, and tech platforms will emerge to the chagrin of those being replaced. Political division will endure, and every step of progress will be sliced in half by a perpetual pendulum blade.

And as long as the Sun continues to rise, 'The People' will keep a-comin'.

PART SIX

ANOTHER CUP OF EARTH

Charles Foster 'Citizen' Kane had his 'Rosebud;' I have the summer of '72 and one early morning in the upper back bedroom of mom's family farmhouse. I was awakened that day by the scent of an approaching rain and the sound of maple tree branches eagerly brushing windows and white clapboard siding.

I raised my head from a feather pillow and rolled out of a cast-iron bed with creaky springs to look for dark clouds, but the breezes had tricked my sense of smell by pushing through old, dusty screens.

I grinned at the weather as I glanced down into the cyclops of a tree-hollow within the maple that had been a maternity room to countless critters. I watched a tire swing with white sidewalls slowly turn like a weathervane with the breezes— then looked up again at a clear-blue sky.

I knew it would be a perfect day.

In 1972, Grandma Aleshire worked at Wright's Hardware Plumbing & Heating in Carthage, Illinois – air conditioning wasn't yet much of a thing. 'Wright's' was painted in cursive on the big front windows of the three-story brick building that had been part of the town's character for 60 years. The Main Street store was on the north side of Courthouse Square in the seat of

Hancock County. Gram, like Grandpa Pickett in Minnesota, would occasionally parlay her job into life lessons by taking me to work with her at the vintage hardware store.

Her boss, Fred Wright, was a short, stout man with a bit of a lisp and a demeanor that varied from jolly to wise. He called every man 'Bud' and most women 'Darlin,' and he'd give me a ride on a floor-to-ceiling ladder with steel wheels that rode on iron pipes from the back to the front of the store. We'd glide past columns of hardwood drawers that were stacked twelve feet high along each side of a thirty-by-ninety-foot room. They were filled with nuts and bolts and thingamajigs and to me back then, the place felt bigger than a Home Depot.

After the ride, Fred would hand me a push broom and "allow" me to sweep the well-seasoned floor with magic crystals that oiled the oak and grabbed dust and dirt at the same time. Fred's summer-school class would get boring soon after the sweep, so I'd stroll across Main Street to begin a self-guided tour around town.

The Hancock County courthouse is a classic building of Indiana Bedford limestone with a roof of red Spanish tile. Lady Justice holds her scales above a white cupola with seven-foot-tall clocks on all four sides. It's as handsome a county courthouse as you'll ever see.

There's a large boulder with a plaque in Courthouse Square that marks the spot where, in October 1858, Stephen Douglas preached the virtues of Popular Sovereignty on a state-by-state basis as the best way to decide the issue of slavery. Eleven days later at the same spot, Abraham Lincoln declared the slave trade to be wrong in every township, county, and state in our divided nation. Douglas won the Senatorial election in 1858. In 1972, the boulder in the square was covered with sparrow droppings.

I was ten years old for half of that year. I wore bib overalls and liked to chew on long weeds in imitation of my idol, Huck Finn, who was from just down the river in Hannibal, Missouri. The bibs cost more than a piece of cloth should have, but they were durable, and Gram justified the expense. Out on the farm, that's all I'd wear. She'd make me add a t-shirt and shoes when we went to town.

As I wandered around Carthage that day, it didn't occur to me that the quaintness of small-town America was in decay. I thought it was just getting old – not on life support, certainly not dead – but I wasn't oblivious to the disappearing landmarks. There was only one restaurant remaining on the square, Grab-A-Snak; JC Penney had closed; Jenkin's Billiard Parlor was turned into a trinket boutique, and the Woodbine Theatre's last picture-show featured a kid in *Wuthering Heights* named Heathrow that Huck Finn and I would have punched in the mouth.

The most critical retailer on the Square – to me – was Ben Franklin's Five-and-Dime, where I could buy penny candy if Gram let Fred Wright pay me a nickel, or if I happened upon a returnable bottle. In '72 Ben was still using bulk buckets of hard candy, gumballs, and jellybeans to tease little boys in overalls.

With no nickel from Fred, and after loitering in the square, I'd occasionally take a three-block walk past a Baptist, a Methodist, then a Presbyterian church to drop in on the Mormon Visitors Center at The Old Carthage Jail site that was across the street from the Catholics' Immaculate Conception.

The Mormons (The Church of Jesus Christ of Latter-Day Saints) landed in Hancock County in 1839 and transformed the tiny town of Commerce into a city half-again bigger than

Chicago. The town sits on a bluff above the Mississippi River where the Illinois border bulges west. The hamlet was renamed Nauvoo (Hebrew for beautiful place) and by 1844 it featured a glorious temple, formidable militia, and a population of 25,000 souls within the 'Metropolitan Statistical Area' of the day.

Those would be Mormon souls, however – a brand the other local Christians didn't understand too well. This led to a fair amount of defamation in county newspapers and as often happens with matters of religion, lack of understanding brought about violence.

The Mormon militia burned some presses, county officials jailed some militia leaders, then an angry mob murdered the Mormon Church founder Joseph Smith and his brother Hyrum in their rooms at the county jail. A few years later a guy named Brigham Young packed up the whole town of Nauvoo and moved it to Utah.

In '72, Mormon elders at the historic site were more than happy to accommodate a curious kid. I took the tour several times and retain a few lessons to this day: a six-panel door has a cross on top and an open bible on the bottom, James of the bible reminds us there are no dumb questions, and angry, intolerant people of all races and creeds destroy and kill unnecessarily.

On my way back toward the miscellaneous stacks of hardware at Wright's, I'd wander alleys in search of a soda bottle then swing by Kibbe's Hancock County Museum. It has since been expanded, but at the time, Gram's cedar chest contained a more comprehensive historical collection.

Fortunately for me in 1972, small-town business owners like Fred Wright – and part-time floor sweepers like me – had lots of flextime and were able to work remotely. He'd load me up in his '58 pickup truck with a wrap-around windshield to drag me out to the county fairgrounds and the city dam on Carthage Lake where we'd share history: he got to remember, and I got to learn.

Independence Day celebrations at the fair once featured pigs on spits, yards of red, white, and blue bunting, three-legged races, and several heats of pacers and trotters at the horse track. In 1972, there was a weenie roast and quarter horse race. Fred gave me a tour of the stables and pointed to a sulky (a one-seat carriage used in harness racing) of my great-grandfather's that was still hanging in the rafters. I secretly wondered if I would inherit it one day.

On the other side of town, where Grandad Aleshire did his business, livestock auctions in Carthage were reduced from twice a week to every other Friday, and people began to suspect Margarite Hopkins at the Sale Barn Café of using a store-bought mix for the gravy on her roast beef sandwiches.

In western Illinois, and across the nation, landscapes were littered with reminders of the previous century: stagnant windmills and oil derricks, piles of by-product from played-out coal mines, deserted homesteads, ravines and hollows strewn with horse-drawn manure spreaders and carbureted automobiles.

The Aleshire farm – 302 acres of stereotypical American family farm – remains down along the banks of Little Creek, on the western edge of the St. Mary's Prairie. The farmhouse was a Prairie Mansion built in 1900. It had a wrap-around porch with a deck on top and by the 1940s, had been modernized with electricity, indoor plumbing and was cooled by the shade of a massive maple. Across the gravel road and a couple acres away from the main house was another, smaller home for the foreman and his family. The farm evolved for 70 years to boast a summer kitchen, garage, chicken coops, two red barns, chutes and corrals, a drive-in scale house, hog feeders, livestock shelters, and several corncribs.

By 1972, the foreman's house was occupied by folks too poor to live in town; the big barn was set for demolition, and the sagging corners of the smaller 'pony barn' spelled its fate just as clearly. The last remaining corncrib was nothing but shade for the swine, and the only weights and measures in the scale house were tons of dust and a wall full of tools to solve challenges that no longer existed. In two April days that year, a bunch of men built a corrugated tin Morton building that would've fit inside the big barn. It replaced them all.

***

All the stores on Courthouse Square, including Wright's Hardware, would close at five o'clock each weekday in 1972, three o'clock on Saturdays, and nothing but church doors were opened on Sunday. After Fred Wright and I had finished our work that day in Carthage, Gram would drive back to the farm on 'hard tops' (paved roads), and on a gravel trail.

She yanked the wheel when a rabbit darted in front of her '69 Ford LTD, but there was a slight thump, and Gram stopped to check on the condition of the unfortunate bunny, then smiled like the Cheshire Cat.

"Perfect. Head shot," she said as she tossed her prey into the trunk. Supper would include another menu item.

Grandad had already taught me how to skin and clean a rabbit – and was way faster at it than I – so he handed me a pail to go search for some berries while he dressed the rabbit and Gram started on gravy that was thick enough to spread with a knife.

On my way back past the cattle pasture to the crick and the hardwood timber where the berries grew, I'd cut through the old drive-in scale house that had become my "Alamo" of farm buildings.

The doors were gone from the cabinet around the old Fairbanks beam scale and the rusted sliders were locked out of balance. The implements of bygone chores in the scale room included curry combs and bridles leftover from the '30s when Mom, Aunty Sis, and Uncle Merle rode their personal horses - Pat, Mike, and Rusty – to their one-room Hickory Flats Schoolhouse. To the east of the scale was a grain bin that once was filled with dusty corn or soybeans. We'd jump and play in the grain as if it were a modern-day ball pit at McDonald's.

My walk back to the crick to fetch berries was about half a mile from the scale house. I'd squeeze between two big doors that by '72 had sagged into the dirt and wouldn't open, then climb a corral fence to stroll down a hundred-yard lane that was lined with a windbreak of Osage orange trees that produced lots and lots of softball-sized fruit called hedge apples. We wondered and tried, but never figured out a useful purpose for the fallen fruit. They were hard, heavy, and so dense the hogs wouldn't even eat them.

The trees were ideal as wind breaks and snow fences, though - short and scraggly with lots of branches – and easy to climb. A year before that trip to the berry patch, my brother Ringo and I climbed up among the hedge apples to lie on branches above a mother sow who decided it was "time" and plopped down in the shade to deliver her piglets. I was fascinated and turned to Ringo at one point and said, "Wow. Mom wasn't lyin'."

"Mom never lies," he replied as he climbed down to save a piglet who was about to be accidentally crushed by the writhing sow. "This is why they want them to be born in the special sheds," he matter-of-factly added as he crawled to the rescue.

The hog feeder lot was a 20-acre rectangle of packed clay with a couple of rain-carved ravines that were miniature imitations of canyon territory out west and perfect for BB gun fights between miniature imitations of TV cowboys. Ringo was at an AAU diving competition in 1972, so he wasn't there to remain undefeated in BB-Gun fights. There was no traumatized sow. There was just me and my pail, and my perfect day.

As I approached a passel of young pigs dining in the feed lot, there was a symphony of clang-shuts from dropped feeder doors they had raised with their snouts. Every pig stopped eating to silently stare at me as if they'd never seen me before… as if I were a stranger who'd just walked into a small-town tavern.

Between the back of the hog lot and the cattle pasture was an orchard that bore no fruit and had become a tangle of trees and sticker-bushes. Foxes and 'coons, quail and snakes would cut through the old orchard, but not a bare-footed boy.

The last quarter mile was on a makeshift road where the only hazards were easy-to-see cowpies and purple thistles. The low-maintenance road dissected the cattle pasture on its way to Holland Cemetery, a site named for the family who first bought the farm after Native Americans vacated the region in the 1820s. Even though we had no family interred there, Grandad, Ringo, and I would occasionally repair the gravestones. The oldest we fixed was from 1836, for a man who knew firsthand of the final conflict in the region between the United States and the Native American Sauk tribe led by Chief Blackhawk in 1832. Mr. Holland's marker has since returned to the earth to join the man, and his combatants.

The cemetery sits about a dozen feet above Little Creek. The hillside next to the graveyard and above the crick isn't tillable but became productive cropland, nonetheless. It's a web of brush and shrubs with enough access to sun, shade, and water to be a perfect berry patch. Blackberries came first in June, followed by raspberries in early July, then gooseberries by August. Mulberries were around for most of the summer, and we had several trees around the house as well. I recall telling my teacher back in Minnesota that we shouldn't sing the song 'Here we go 'round the mulberry bush' because it was wrong. "There's no mulberry bushes," I'd insist, "they're trees!"

I picked enough blackberries for the three of us, left a few ripe ones for the birds, then hiked up my overalls and crawled down the bank to wade in the creek. It was knee deep on a ten-year-old and moved along quickly enough for a couple of bark chunk races from the rapids to the fallen tree bridge that doubled as a finish line.

After the races I'd scoop tadpoles to see if any had legs yet, then I'd stroll back to the farmhouse in pant legs that were still rolled up, and wet, for a meal of pan-fried chicken and rabbit that tasted the same, green beans from the garden, and Gram's gravy over white bread - followed by a bowl of cream and those berries.

After supper, Gram would freshen a deck of playing cards with talcum powder for a few games of 3-handed Pitch, then later, I'd stroll out to the big maple tree for a game of 'Swoop' on the tire swing.

There were no siblings, or cousins around to give me an "Underdog" on the swing, so I'd compete with myself. I'd climb a stepladder as far as I could with the tire hooked in my arm, then launch out over a playing field of toys that varied in size and shape from a baby doll to a wooden alphabet block, to the plastic army man we called "laying down guy" who was worth the most points if scooped in a swoop. Points were compiled based on the number and size of items one could collect within three passes of the white-side-walled tire over the playing field. I won every game.

At the farm, we were never told when it was time to go to bed. We always just knew – and after the sun had set on the clear blue sky, my perfect day would conclude the way it had begun, with my head on a feather pillow in a creaky, cast-iron bed.

***

Twenty-five years later, on November 18, 1997 – long after my strolls past hedge apples and the miracle of life to a patch of berries – the antebellum allusions of the Aleshire farmhouse were crushed by a backhoe, then – like Charles Foster Kane's "Rosebud" – reduced to ashes to make more room for the future. It was the melancholiest day of my life. I felt wimpy and turned away from Mary Beth to keep her from seeing my tears when I told her, "They tore down the farmhouse today." She spun me around and gave me the best hug I ever had.

Later that night, I got to thinking of how – sometime in the 70s – Industrial Aged Hancock County had become "Historic," as in "ago," "prior," since," "gone by." Carthage College ran off to Kenosha, a local girl named Colleen's 'Miss Illinois' banner was fading in a cedar chest, Thompson's General Store in St. Mary was all out of Ethyl gasoline, soda pop, and front windows. Trains stopped stopping in Hancock County.

I made a habit somewhere along the line, of tempering emotional losses of friends, family, and landscapes with reminders of the existence and experiences of preceding generations. To American Indians, "Industrial" was the least welcome of Ages, and 1972 was one in a hundred and fifty years of degeneration.

There's a saying among the former tribes of the region: "Let me go back and take one drink more from the old spring."

The current in Little Creek varies from raging torrent to couldn't-raise-a-nightcrawler. Not far from the berry patch are the remnants of a berm that once was a bridge for the stagecoach that carried Lincoln and Douglas to Courthouse Square. Farther down the line, after spilling into the LaMoine River, the little crick makes anonymous, cup-by-cup donations of topsoil to the great Mississippi Delta.

A 'New Age' perpetuates technological and physical change in counties with no Interstate highways. Addresses beginning with 'www' replace rural fire numbers, and Courthouse Square in Carthage has been revived with resilience, bits, bytes, and URLs where there once was hardware, durability, and *The County Journal*.

By the end of the 20th century, the souls of Indian chiefs and 19th century industrialists had colluded to create the communal economics of modern farming. The land that is the Aleshire and neighboring farms would be picked clean of buildings and landmarks. Fences, corrals, and loading chutes were pulled, hedgerows yanked, and service lanes tilled in an apparent challenge to the sons and daughters of the computerized millennium to do what they may with this place, to create their own definition of a perfect day.

The irony is lost in a cycle. The Potawatomi hunters and gatherers were not the beginning of Hancock County any more than the oil-burning independent farmer is its end.

Progress and evolution find every corner of the globe, often taking two steps back for every three forward. Somewhere in the process, the ages and eras, the causes and concerns, become melded into one more cup of earth.

PART SEVEN

EXODUS

My sister Jenny invited me to join her on a short bus that made its way around Burnsville, Minnesota back in the '70s. The classic rig was from the '50s and looked like a modified version of Ms. Frizzle's "Magic School Bus."

In place of the wings and colorful decals, it had rust and riveted slabs of hand-painted sheet metal, and rather than the words 'Wahoo!' or 'Blast Off!' in the destination plate; "Crystal Lake Baptist Church" was spelled out on each side beneath the windows.

The bus crusaded from the little church that sits at the foot of Lindsay Vonn's Buck Hill Ski 'Resort' and made rounds like an ice cream truck through the neighborhood with the constant creak of springs and struts evangelizing in place of a redundant tune.

I was using a shabby Sherwood hockey stick to add tennis ball stains to the garage door of home number seven on Scott Street in Burnsville Heights when the bus stopped one Sunday for Jenny.

"Wanna go too?" she asked.

I shrugged, tossed the Sherwood between the garages, and within an hour was in a Sunday School class memorizing the books of the Bible, playing church games, and listening to a kid named Jim Vagle belt out adult hymns with a child's vocal cords.

A trip on the short bus set in motion an exploration of faith that would carry me through a labyrinth of thought and purpose that was singular to me yet interconnected with the entire universe.

Both sets of grandparents were Baptists, but the only thing they shared with the Crystal Lake congregation was Jesus and uncomfortable pews. The Baptist Picketts religiously attended weekly service at a stoic, north-urban church while the Aleshires did chores on a farm; they attended a semi-southern Baptist church for the Easter resurrection, and whenever a local mortal died.

Our parents didn't claim a particular faith and rarely went to church but, like Pontius Pilot, didn't find any fault in it. They had a laisse-fare approach to redemption. Pop believed in a Creator because "there was too much evidence not to." This was enough to bless him with a remarkably peaceful hospice at home.

During my final visit, I read a few Psalms for him and asked how he felt about the afterlife. He cracked a cagy grin and said, "Do I look worried?"

Pop had stared down years of toil and trouble, and nurtured laughter, joy, and the pursuit of wisdom all the while. He quietly, and matter-of-factly said farewell to me with a pleasantly smug statement of confidence that was a tidy summary of a lifetime of life lessons and a reminder to take a deep breath, relax, and be thankful. I cherish that moment.

Mom was as skeptical about religion as dad was frugal. She claimed to be a Latter Day Jew. This was 40 years before a guy named H. Alan Scott turned the phrase into a testimonial and stand-up comedy act. She would often warn us to "be wary of God-fearin' Christians and circles of prayer." Her conflicted declaration of faith was a challenge, like Lieutenant Dan yelling at God.

I heard a familiar refrain while Mary Beth and I were standing in a vestibule outside the priest's offices at Nativity of Our Lord Catholic Church awaiting our marriage interview with monsignor Clarence Steiner.

Pastor Patrick Lannan's door was open, and we couldn't help but hear him dismiss a wealthy parishioner and her threats about the direction of the parish. She left in a huff and Lannan stepped from his office into the hallway. He offered a blessing, bade her good-bye, then looked at me and said, "be wary of overly-pious people, kid."

"This guy is a real closer," I thought. "When did he meet my mom?"

Father Lannan may have been the closer in 1989, but what sold me on the Catholic Faith was the magnitude of exhaustive theology. Mary Beth never made a single inference to me about converting, and even after reading centuries of philosophical analysis from scores of brilliant minds, I didn't sign up for another eight years, after Mary Murphy entered day care and we became immersed in church and school involvement.

To me, the active commitment of parishioners at Nativity echoed the Catholic church's status as the largest charitable network on earth. At Nativity, I could feel the philosophies of Thomas Aquinas, Catherine of Siena, Francis of Assisi, and Rene Descartes' linking of truths. I sensed G. K. Chesterton, Bishop Sheen, Fr. Spitzer, and the challenges to unjust patriarchy by Mary Daly and the local Sisters of St. Joseph, as well.

My time on the pastoral council coincided with the pinnacle of the priest scandals in Minnesota that divided, drove wedges, and brought many together in frustration, shame, and prayers for both victims and perpetrators that seemed to conflict, but were consistent with the painful and redeeming forgiveness of Christ.

Prior to the commitment to Catholicism, I had a serious relationship with Lutherans who shared wonderful youth programs and - at Augsburg College - taught me how to study the humanities. As I was learning to learn, several Jewish kids of St. Louis Park, MN who were co-workers at a lumber yard, then friends, gave me insights into their faith and worldviews. Unloading a 52-foot semi-trailer of fiberglass insulation on a hot August day brings faiths together.

I know more than most about Mormons due to frequent trips to visitors' centers where founders Joseph and Hyrum Smith were murdered in Carthage, Illinois and up the road to Nauvoo – the town that would be Salt Lake City if not for the murders.

My childhood was sprinkled with incidental Catholic mass experiences as well, following Saturday sleepovers with friends who 'had to go.' The Brinkhaus boys were required to grab a bulletin as a reverse ticket stub of proof to Mary, their mother, and Paul Wallace was tough as leather on a playground, but one of those kids who seemed to understand the peace of faith in church while the rest of us fidgeted.

I loved the Baptists growing up, because they loved me, and I appreciate the Presbyterians because of a baptism at Oak Grove Church back in 1961. I believe that's where I was assigned at least one Guardian Angel – a source of universal truth that would guide me when I was listening and deliver "character-building" lessons when I wasn't. Evidently, characters take a long time to build.

I was listening one time in San Francisco. In 1984, a friend at a Minneapolis publishing house convinced me to take a sabbatical – to blow off my career path – and go work for him on a ring crew at horse shows up and down the coast of the once-Golden State. We had a break in our schedule after two weeks in Bakersfield, so I hopped on a Greyhound and headed to the 'City by the Bay' to surprise a transplanted college friend.

Risk for reward was a common practice in America back before technology gave us all too much information too quickly; before we padded the pain of discovery and issued rewards without effort; before we mashed all the souls into a complicit paste. Back in '84, my risk to surprise worked in reverse, and I got another lesson.

"Had a wild hair. Off to Seattle for a few days. Leave a message," my would-be host, Jill's, answering machine said as she went off on a spontaneous adventure of her own.

I closed my eyes, tilted my head back and shook it, then looked up to bounce my options off the ceiling of the Transbay Bus Terminal. I didn't know another soul in San Francisco and had already purchased a train ticket to Santa Barbara. I decided to see a few sites that afternoon then head south in the morning.

I reached down for the satchel at my feet to see nothing but shoelaces. A thief had stolen the bag containing a change of clothes, my journal, a hundred dollars, and a lucky horseshoe that was to be a gift for my friend. This left me with $13 dollars and the train ticket that, fortunately, was in my back pocket.

The YMCA had not yet dropped its association with Christian Men, so I took the advice of the Village People and got a $5 room at the Embarcadero branch before setting off on an $8 exploration of one of the nation's most expensive cities.

I didn't meet God at the Powell & Market Cable Car turnaround but, among the mass of transient and bewildered humanity, I met a woman who said she could introduce me to Him through the teachings of an enlightened reverend named Sun Myong Moon.

She was a natural beauty who, in the age of 'Big Hair,' wore hers naturally. She looked deep into my eyes with every statement and seductively promised we could have a great time that very night at a mansion party packed with young people just like us.

"Do they take train tickets?" I asked.

"Money is irrelevant," she replied.

I wasn't a math major and didn't know much about the reverend's Unification Church, but I did know that within three minutes, girls who looked like her didn't look at guys like me, like that. I figured money was gonna get relevant at a Berkeley mansion and opted to let the would-be Circes lure a more heroic figure to her island.

My guardian either took a break, or I stopped listening again when I invested half of my remaining eight dollars on whiskey and spent the evening loitering around the Embarcadero near The Y, where I chatted with an old hobo who told me tales of glory days riding the rails with no point of departure, and no ETA.

The five-dollar room was like a miniature dorm on an Eastern Bloc campus. It had chipped plaster, a lumpy cot, a sink with no water supply, and a square portal of a window. I awoke to a view of the Golden Gate Bridge and shared my disappointment about its appearance with the desk clerk.

"Buy a map, shit-kicker," he said.

The YMCA overlooks the Oakland-Bay Bridge, which is impressive in its largesse and functionality, but no Golden Gate. I didn't have enough money for a map, but I could always afford to listen and learn. The diversity of skin hues and characters in California came in greater volume than I'd ever experienced, but that wasn't intimidating.

Several moves over the years introduced me to a lot of personality types and reinforced one of Pop's lectures: "you don't have to be exposed to all kinds of people to have respect and personal integrity."

Some wear a cross, a star of David, or one with a crescent. Some praise Brahma or Buddha. Some deny the spirits altogether, but each has a faith of some degree or decree. Even atheists have faith in bridges.

A cable car clangs and a short bus creaks. Baptists await the second coming, Jews the first. Presbyterians know it's imminent, Muslims that it will only happen once, Buddhists that it's endless, and Catholics ask Mary for help along the way.

Every route, every mortal journey arrives at a terminal with a universal conclusion. Be it heaven or hell or nothing at all; we reap just what we sow.

PART EIGHT

THE CLEAN PLATE CLUB

My Pop pulled some strings and got me into the commercial dishwashing trade back in the early '70s. I was only ten years old, so it was a lot like when Mozart's dad got him into the music business.

Pop was creating options for his multi-talented son as granddad Aleshire was training me in another field. Gramps handed me a shovel one day and said, "Here, stick this in the ground," then followed up with, "Good, now you'll never be out of work."

My prodigious ditch-digging and plate scraping abilities never got beyond part-time vocation, but the dishwashing skillset did become a cog in the wholeness of my life journey. It led me to service, sacrifice, delusions of grandeur and, ultimately, to humble reconciliation.

Pop was a sucker for clean-and-tidy and encouraged dutiful commitment to the noble order of dishwashers. He said there's always dignity in doing something nobody else wants to do, and that if a kid with soggy socks could smile and scour, and spray the remnants of other people's pleasure, he would build character and could smile just about anywhere.

On December 31, 1975, my buddy Bruce Michelsen and I were the only two soggy-socked kids on the planet willing to be dignified by the dish room at the Corner House Restaurant in Burnsville, Minnesota.

The building was a repainted relic of a structure that was nestled in the wetlands of the Minnesota River Valley. It was built in the 1920s and evolved like an unplanned Lego project 'til it became a 1960s country supper club called The Embassy that featured a portico façade with heroic Greek columns adorned with flags of multiple nations.

By the time it became The Corner House, the portico had been artfully transformed into a pagoda and the menu added Chinese fare to the steak and starch, but direct access had been eliminated when Lyndale Avenue – ol' Highway 65 – became state-of-the-art Interstate-35. This redirected travelling peddlers and crooner-loving couples to consume their cigarettes, steaks, and Old Fashioneds at joints near exit ramps on a strip of freeway a few miles north in Bloomington.

The river valley was once home to Chief Black Dog and his band of Mdewankanton Sioux, but there was no flag for their nation at The Embassy. In 1965, new political leadership brought a different vision - in the form of a garbage dump - to the marshy lowlands that surrounded the diplomatic restaurant. There was little objection from new residents who added to the desecration with refuse by the truck load.

The site was ill-advised for a restaurant, let alone teenaged dishwashers – even before it became toxic. Most of the basin is a natural flood plain and the land had been submerged in fresh water several times in preceding decades.

On the day of the eve of 1976, a thaw turned the lot behind The Corner House into a sloppy mess that had begun to freeze by happy hour. The icy coat couldn't mask the acres of refuse next door, and wafting aromas hung in the air like leftover mistletoe in the lounge. Indigenous wildlife in the valley had come to be outnumbered by the type of undomesticated animals that are drawn to garbage dumps like martini-swilling peddlers of the era were drawn to roadside liquor lounges.

Bruce and I were oblivious to how – and how far – the site had degenerated. We embedded ourselves into the modern ecosystem for a buck sixty-five an hour and were pre-occupied with immediate conditions. The hot water heater had failed, and the sinks were plugged beyond the reaches of desperate coat hangers. We did our best to clean dishes, glasses, and utensils in stainless steel kettles filled with cold, soapy water that we'd haul to the back lot. We'd shoo scurrying rodents before adding a few more gallons of sewage to the embattled environment.

We smiled, and cussed, and laughed, and endured the evening – only to get stiffed for $11.55 each. Like the smattering of customers who dined from dubious dishware, our fortunes were ambiguous. A few months later, after a mysterious fire, the building would join rubber tires and checks in the landfill.

Our usual cohort, Scott "Pube" Huberty, somehow avoided that character-building opportunity; probably because his standards were above polluted sanctuaries. He landed us a high-class gig at a dinner theatre and music lounge: Marco Polo Supper Club. Teasing rats were replaced by barely-adult servers in alluring black-and-white waitress outfits who loved to taunt pubescent teenagers. They'd show cleavage and reach for things beyond the humility of their polyester skirts to give us uncomfortable pause as we processed dish-laden bus carts that arrived in waves for six or seven hours.

Summertime warms the air in Minnesota, and dish rooms become northern, all-inclusive resorts to house flies who flock to the sauna conditions and pools of all-you-can-eat leftovers. When we weren't being taunted by grownup girls, we'd revert to little boy games.

Bruce devised a fly killing contest that we tracked with pencil tallies on a towel dispenser. One point for a swat kill, two for a wet towel snap, and five for a sweeping, bared-handed snag. Twenty points was an Ace, forty a Blue Max... I was the Red Baron and had more than fifty points one night when owner Milo came in for a spot inspection. He spied the scoreboard and jumped to a conclusion.

"What the hell's going on? He begged. "I can't afford this! How can you break that many dishes?"

"That's our fly-killing competition," I explained in a complaining voice loud enough to be heard over the din and clatter of dishes and power-washing machines.

"Oh..." he said as his eyes darted around the room at the invaders who were buzzing our realm like Messerschmitts over Great Britain in 1940.

"And your tie clashes..." I added in a tone that implied we weren't getting the love and dignity worthy of our commitment.

He had to tolerate our occasional insubordination. We showed up to a place nobody else wanted to be and, thanks to Scott's incredibly high standards, didn't leave until the sweatbox was spic-and-span, and actually looked a bit dignified.

As a lead-up to the dynamic dish room trio, I worked at the three Sweden House Smorgasbord restaurants that our parents purchased from Pop's former employer, International Multifoods. My first-ever paid gig, however, was on Sunday mornings at eatery number four, Pickett's family restaurant in

Rosemount, Minnesota. That's where Pop must have paid local authorities to look the other way from child labor laws. I got paid a dollar per day - and was told by mom to keep it quiet. I've since learned my indentured siblings got nothing - and liked it.

The small-town venue was the favorite of the family's eateries. My folks bonded with locals as Mom charmed cops, business owners, and a handful of Minnesota Viking football players who frequented the joint for free coffee and her engaging ability to 'hold forth' in conversation.

But Mom passed, and the restaurants closed. A few years later some high school buddies and I got pulled over by Rosemount deputy sheriff, Ray McNamara, during a joyride on the outskirts of town. He took our beer, told me he wouldn't call the ol' man if I went straight home, then said, "We all sure miss your Ma."

I went straight home.

I got a real job at a lumber yard to help pay for college, and decided that, despite my incredible knack for removing hardened gravy from ladle handles, baked-on cheese and onion from stoneware crocs, and every spec of egg yolk from every single fork tine, sometimes one had to let go of God's obvious gifts to explore new horizons. Plus, by the age of twelve, I figured out it's more fun to be on the pleasurable, dish dirtying side and wanted nothing to do with the kitchens of the restaurant industry.

Want and duty are often two different things. After Mom and the restaurants were gone, Pop took up with a new division of Ecolab called ESS. It was an early adaptation of outsourcing, where the company would hire and manage dish room employees to take the hassle off the plates of restauranteurs.

When Pop got into a staffing jam, or needed my keen instincts, he'd call me up to fill a slot. We'd drive around the tougher parts of town in a 12-passenger van to pick up employees who were usually on hard times or trying to make a new start.

We'd creep up alleys where I'd hop out and go knock on a side window or whistle 3 times to let my co-workers know it was friend, not foe, who came beckoning with opportunity and a bus ride to dignity. I come from a family that knows all about hard times and new starts, but I learned from my ESS brothers in soggy socks that there's a whole 'nother level of toughness and perseverance.

I was fortunate enough to discover new opportunities and avoid the kitchen side of the industry for many years, but my expertise had a calling back to the dish room during Men's Club Lenten fish fries at our church. More than a thousand faithful "Mackerel Snappers" would visit the school cafeteria for humble meals of fish and chips – with lots of tartar sauce and ketchup.

I'd join soulmates like Kevin, Morgan, Scott, and Dan and we'd welcome future dignitaries like Boy Scouts Peter Howard and Tommy Hedman to make sure the cup holder squares had no rings of tartar or tomato in the towers of plastic school lunch trays.

Civic and patriotic duty made its call as well. Serving Our Troops (SOT) is a St. Paul-based organization dedicated to honoring the sacrifices of Minnesota's National Guard, the 34th Red Bull Infantry Division. The honoring group is led by a guy named Pat Harris, who has enlisted, motivated, and deployed enough volunteers to form his own Division. They've served more than 100,000 steak dinners in St. Paul, Iraq, Kuwait, Croatia, Norway, and at bases throughout the U.S.

St. Paul's legendary Mancini's Char House is a primary supporter and the family donated space and staff during hours they would typically be closed, to host a big screen, virtual-link meal for families at home and soldiers who had an extended deployment in Kuwait. The event was a daytime maneuver, and I observed dirty plates and pans that were amassing for a five o'clock ambush of an unsuspecting comrade of soggy socks – Mancini's night-time dishwasher.

I instinctively followed my training and fired up the Hobart machine to out-flank the hordes of dishware. One of the Mancini brothers happened by and gave me a dignified wink of thanks that was as good as a medal.

Life has a way of bringing false visions back to reality. That garbage dump in Burnsville was revealed as a disastrous error in science and judgment, and delusions of grandeur regarding my dishwashing career were revealed as well. The awakening began as soon as I started seeking acknowledgement. You know how it is. You do something that's supposed to remain between you, your conscience, and God – then you erase the deed by bragging about it, and what a swell person you are.

I expected recognition in the dumbest place possible – my own kitchen. I got to thinking Mary Beth was taking for granted that I would do the dishes just because she did 98% of the cooking, and I made it a point to remind her of my exalted dish room status.

"I've been washing dishes since I was ten years old," I pontificated. "I've washed more dishes, pots, and pans than you will ever touch or see."

"Yeah?..." she said as she threw a dish towel in my face, "... and your statue is gonna be right next to the Tin Man's in the town square."

In 2013, my nomination to the Dishwashing Hall of Fame disappeared into a stack of white plates covered with shrink wrap in the corner of a restaurant surplus store. During my final visit with Pop, we chatted about a lot of memories, and I brought up my Sunday morning shift in the Rosemount dish room. He threw his head back with his dentured smile then bowed his head in a chuckle before looking up to grin.

"Oh, my, yes I remember!" he laughed. "You were the slowest dishwasher to ever work a sprayer!"

His laugh mellowed to a reflective grin as he paused to add, "But… you never left a bit of egg yolk on a single fork tine."

A little character-building, a little dignity, and the plates are clean.

PART NINE

GLADYS AND BOB

Bruce Michelsen and I were 13 years-old and all dialed in to listen to an original recording of Orson Welles' 1938 broadcast: *The War of the Worlds*. When it first aired, the radio adaptation of the classic book by H. G. Wells (no relation) terrified thousands of people throughout the country who believed it was a live newscast and that Martians were really invading Grover's Mill, New Jersey.

Bruce was on his twin bed running the machine, I was just below on a pull-out trundle, and we were fired up. His mom made us popcorn and poured soda-pop over ice cubes in plastic highballs. His dad figured we were old enough for gun safety, so he could trust us with a marvelous 'toy' he'd kept stashed away – a vintage reel-to-reel tape recorder that looked like it was used in Film Noir by a hard-boiled detective with a pretty girlfriend.

Bruce threaded then tightened the tape with a spin of his finger in the receiving reel, turned a big plastic knob, and the throaty voice of Orson Welles began to speak over crackling magnetic tape. The Martians were at Grover's Mill… but we never made it that far. The sounds of a quacking duck-call stole the show.

Older brother Dave beat Bruce to the machine that day and had been practicing to sound like a mallard so he could sneak up on one when the season was right. Bruce desperately searched through squiggling sounds of fast-forwarded tape, to no avail; the quacking went on for at least an hour, and another slice of the Golden Age of Radio had been wiped from memory.

Dave wasn't the first to erase history – or to change it. Newspapers have been using headlines to exaggerate forever with headlines like "Blood Thirsty Spaniards" that started the Spanish-American War in 1898. They told us the Titanic was sinking, but no lives were lost, that Dewey defeated Truman, and – the day after Orson Welles' broadcast – newspapers across the land used sensational headlines to turn a handful of curious callers into an urban myth with: "Radio Play Terrorizes Nation." We like our history to be what we want to hear – or something utterly fantastic.

Few people have seen more history than Bruce's parents, Robert Frederick and Gladys Anderson Michelsen. They were married when Eisenhower was president of the United States, and they were born when Paul von Hindenburg was president of Germany.

A year prior to the mythical Martian invasion, Hindenburg's namesake airship famously crashed and burned at Lakehurst, New Jersey in a foreshadow of what would happen to his successor, Adolph Hitler… and to the little green men at Grover's Mill.

On the other side of the globe, airships were exploding and the invasion of mainland China was very real as the island-bound people of Japan set out to build an Asian Empire. They had divine certainty in their emperor's new war, along with an 800-year winning streak to back up their beliefs.

The United States got involved after Pearl Harbor in 1941, and Bob Michelsen became a "guest" of the emperor for five months in 1945 before the Japanese winning streak would end. He was a 'blister' gunner on a B-29 Superfortress that was shot down over Tokyo, and the surviving crew was imprisoned in the Imperial stables (now the East Gardens) where they were blind-folded for interviews conducted with the international language of saliva, sticks, and clubs.

Bob left Japan from Omori Prison Camp in Tokyo Bay, alongside notables like 'Pappy' Boynton, and Lou Zamperini, whose incredible journey was shared through the book, *Unbroken,* by Laura Hillenbrand, then a movie by the same name. For Bob Michelsen, the memories of prison life, hunger, filth, and the 'interviews' have endured for more than 75 years. Thoughts of his crew and prison mates have revisited him almost 30,000 times – at least once for each day.

Back in Minnesota, Gladys Anderson had survived polio and was enduring the war's uncertainty as she anonymously contributed to the effort as chlorophyll does to a flamboyant lily. The officer who would liberate her future husband was a Naval Commander named Harold Stassen of Minnesota who had resigned as the state's governor to join the forces allied to defend liberty.

The couple married in the 1950s and were pursuing their American dreams on Myrtle Drive, a suburban cul-de-sac in Burnsville, when I met their son, Bruce, in 1970. He was a lot like me, part jock, part nerd. The difference was, Bruce embraced his Nerd with radio-controlled airplanes, amateur film making, and learning to train champion field dogs from his dad. My dad was plenty busy with seven kids, four restaurants, and a wife with cancer, so I freeloaded on Bruce's enterprise, and on the Michelsens' hospitality. They opened their home to let me come and go like a feral cat with a curiosity for stability.

Meeting Bruce came with a bonus: his best friend Scott Huberty, who shared the airplanes with Bruce and model-railroading with his father. Together, we were a three-legged stool of pals who functioned in a space somewhere between cool and geeky. I, being the loose peg, wasn't very good at either, but we were all fortunate to grow up with kids like the ones who thought Ferris Bueller was a righteous dude. In the class of '79 at Burnsville High School – and, for me, at my eventual alma mater in Rosemount – our "sportos, motorheads, geeks, bloods, waistoids, dweebies, and dickheads" had lots of cross-over and remain close-knit friends to this day.

Bruce placed Scott in charge of cinematography when he launched his film career in the mid-70s. He had the financial backing of a powerful media magnate, John Cowles Jr., owner and publisher of the Minneapolis afternoon *Star* and morning *Tribune* newspapers. Cowles gave Bruce exclusive distribution rights on Vivian, Marian, and Myrtle Drives.

As tail-end Baby-boomers, we were raised on cowboy tales that would give way to spaceman stories, that would give way to lawyer and cop dramas, that would give way to fantastical accounts of beautiful, brilliant women who could out-think and beat up burly men. Five-foot-nine, 150-pound Gene Autry used to do the same thing in his musical westerns back in the '30s. Hollywood is cyclical; except for the constant projection of gore and violence that just won't go away.

Young Michelsen's production, *They called Us Dirt & Grime* (I was Grime) was classic 20th century 'Old West' with the requisite clichés of grubby cowboys eating tin plates of beans served by saloon women wearing garters. Suburbia is short on

68

horses, so we rode stick ponies, and we'd remove the Curtis-Mathes TV from the indoor sets - for historical accuracy. Tight budgets would force Scott to emulate the great John Ford with single-take shots from a hand-held Kodak Super-8.

Bruce remained in the film industry for decades. He was a peddler of cameras, lenses, and peripherals until the digitized cell phones of the Tech Age sent his career to a cedar chest filled with prints by Kodak and Polaroid.

Our childhood adventures were empowered by Gladys and Bob, and millions of "Greatest Generation" parents like them who nurtured our imaginations while wars raged, economies ebbed and flowed, politicians lied, and bureaucracies discriminated. Gladys and Bob embraced inclusions that had never before occurred. They held tight to conservative discipline – without political agenda, or government mandate. They liberally opened their home to a feral cat like me with no formal invitation or declaration – simply because they saw a need and cared.

'Great' to Americans is a term that is usually excessive, even when accurate. With the Michelsens, it is an understatement in the same way that humility outweighs conceit.

It's easy for us sophisticated citizens of the New Age to roll our eyes and shake our heads at ancestors – some still alive – who believed mortals could be divine, or that Martians could invade – and that they'd pick New Jersey. We have the benefit of cancellation, of erased tapes, and folks like Gladys and Bob, who waked for tens of thousands of days in a row, to think of others before themselves.

PART TEN

THE SPIRIT OF '76

"If you quit when you suck, you'll suck forever."

- Mori Calliope

I once had a sacred spot with a big round rock at the base of a tree on a hill. It sat on a glacial ridge above the Minnesota River in Burnsville. The nature-made chair was flat on top and had a panoramic view of metropolitan Minneapolis and Saint Paul from about a dozen miles south. I'd climb there to gaze at a vista that spanned from the Cathedral of St. Paul in the east, past the skyline of Minneapolis, then on to the world's first indoor shopping center in Edina.

The view from Burnsville is one of the best in our metro. There's an even better one on the same ridge in nearby Mendota Heights. It sits 250 feet above the confluence of the Minnesota and Mississippi rivers and is so good it has a plaque. Riverboat captains started calling it 'Pilot Knob' in the mid-19th century, long after the Dakota, Ojibwe, and Iowa peoples called the sacred spot Oheyawahi, "a hill much visited," for ten thousand years.

In 1851 the tribes sold Oheyawahi, and 25 million acres, to the Bureau of Indian Affairs in exchange for annual interest income on an oxymoron – a 'government trust' of 1.4 million dollars. The BIA officials put the 'bureau' in bureaucrats and lore has it they inspired Bernie Madoff. In the end, the tribes and I made out about the same; we didn't see anything. Developers took my hill in 1977, built an apartment building, and rented out my "Spectacular View" for $249 a month. Forty-five years later, I can see Oheyawahi from the den window in our apartment across the river in St. Paul that we rent for ten times the cost of the spectacular view. The tribes still see nothing.

The first time I arrived at the spot was by accident, and I had little empathy for 31,000 generations of preceding Natives. It was all about me. I was 13 and walking, so I must have had a blown bike tire. This was the summer of '74, six months after we moved back into the house on Upton Avenue – the landing pad that reestablished Minnesota as our home in 1970. It burned in March of '71 and sat charred and vacant for months as the scales of justice regarding the cause of the fire ticked and tocked like a metronome.

Pop and older brother Ringo spent evenings and weekends rebuilding the house. My contribution was to soak old bathroom tiles in 5-gallon buckets, wipe off the smoke and soot, then chip adhesive off the back with a hammer and chisel so they could be reused. Pop paid me a nickel a tile. My brother got room and board.

After returning to Upton, it seemed as though the storms of the previous three years had passed. All signs of the fire were gone – except the mis-matched shingles on the roof where the fire burned through, and the deformed plastic frame on a TV set that melted but could still pick up all five channels: PBS, CBS, NBC, ABC, and Metro-Media 11.

In 1974, the five oldest kids were back to part-time work at our family's four restaurants, and after a trip to Oklahoma to see her favorite cousins, the effects of cancer treatments seemed to be waning, and Mom had a different energy and looked a lot better.

I don't know where I was headed when I discovered the spot, only that it felt as if a guardian had guided me there. Everyone who's driven north through Burnsville on I-35 has experienced the 'wow' factor of cresting the ridge for the first time. My spot had a wider lens, a peaceful solitude, and a built-in chair. As panoramic urban views go, it's up there with Mulholland Drive in Los Angeles, the Duquesne Overlook in Pittsburgh, or New York City from the Statue of Liberty – in a humble, midwestern kind of way.

Based on its strategic potential, I figure The Spot went into use not long after climate change chased glaciers back up into Canada and the first humans arrived. The round flat rock was so perfectly positioned that I wondered if a thoughtful Indian dragged it there centuries before and if some kid my age had been guided there too, but thought it was boring because there were no water towers or buildings to trigger memories of a nomadic childhood.

I had plenty of triggers. I didn't really know how to critically think or reflect at the time, or to pray, so I'd climb there to remember what I'd learned so far, to wonder, and to hope. The farthest landmark was the water tower in New Hope, 170 blocks northwest, where my cousins lived in suburbs that were all built up and the only green spaces were square city parks. One hundred blocks north was my grandparents' apartment and the Washburn water tower of domed concrete that – with its rock-solid men and their swords – looked like a tomb for a medieval knight; it wasn't far from an abandoned trolley bridge across Minnehaha Creek where we we'd climb around with an abundant lack of caution.

It was only 30 blocks to the radio towers of WDGY and Bloomington's Nine Mile Creek where Jimmy Brinkhaus would flip rocks and I'd grab scurrying crawdads. Nearby, at the bottom of the ridge, was the old Savage swing bridge where we'd look for loose railroad spikes; it spanned a flood plain where we'd spear carp when the spring thaw and rains brought ugly fish into waist-deep waters.

As jet airplanes came and went from the international airport, I'd sit on the rock and think of the places I'd go if I ever got to fly. I'd remember field trips to mystical St. Paul to see golden horses atop the State capitol, Winter Carnival ice castles, Fighting Saints hockey in an arena with see-through boards, and expeditions to bag doughnuts at the Highway building with Grandpa Pickett. This hill I had discovered would become a back-up to my most favorite hill down at the farm.

When I left the new sacred spot after my first visit, I knew I'd be back, but had no idea that each call would be made by a boy unrecognizable to his former self.

***

Home number eleven came along out of nowhere to me. I was of an age that they – the grownups – thought it best to shelter me and the 'Little Girls' - my two younger sisters, Missy and Andi – from unpleasantry. I was told when to do homework, when it was time to eat, and when to start packing. I would be notified when a loved one was about to – or had already – died.

Our new 'home' was two apartments across the hall from each other. It was 1975 by now and after an oil embargo, historic stagflation, and medical expenses, the financial well was running dry for our folks. All four restaurants were closed, Mom was in bed or in a wheelchair most of the time, and we learned that cancer made Grandad Aleshire's insides look as hopeless as the decaying buildings on his farm. The grown-ups kept functioning in "that's life" mode, so I did, too.

My room was next door to our parents', and I once caught sight of Mom with no shirt – and no breasts – just gauze from armpits to waist. I knew they didn't want me to see that. She smiled and said, "go get me some water, would you please, honey?"

They didn't know what I could take, and what I couldn't. I wanted to show I could be tough and caring. To prove that I could take it, no matter what 'it' was. I wanted to say, "Mommy, let me help," but just went to fetch the water.

When I returned, Mom was in her pajamas acting like it was any old Sunday afternoon. She asked how my civics project was coming along and if I had written to Senator Hubert Humphrey in Washington as she had instructed.

Mom and Dad knew the Humphreys. Dad's parents helped Hubert get elected to his first office as Mayor of Minneapolis in the '40s, and he was in the U.S. Senate when Mom's speed and savvy got her a call-up from the steno pool to type for Vice President Nixon and former First Lady, Eleanor Roosevelt.

This was before my parents met in Washington DC or had any idea they'd be constituents of the future vice president. After moving to Minnesota, Mom and Dad, along with my grandparents, left Lyndon Johnson and the Democrats over Vietnam and the well-intentioned but ill-conceived 'Great Society' program. They became active in the GOP and, ironically, were key organizers for Humphrey's senatorial opponent, Clark McGregor in 1970 – this was back when political foes could discuss policy and remain friends.

On Independence Day 1970, we were watching a parade on Bloomington's Lyndale Avenue when mom spotted Hubert and Muriel approaching in a convertible. We were sitting in front of a florist shop and mom ran in and bought a rose. As their car crept past, she had me take the flower to Mrs. Humphrey. They spotted Mom, flashed their signature smiles, and waved emphatically. Muriel blew us a kiss.

In 1974, the Humphreys, Ed Asner, and All-Star Wrestling champ, Verne Gagne, were at our reconditioned Upton Avenue home for a premiere party to launch the movie 'The Wrestler' that was produced by close family friend, Bill Frank Jr.

In 1975, I received a personal note from Mr. Humphrey along with a large manilla envelope stuffed with information about our constitution, how laws were passed, and the separations of power. I got an A.

In 1975, Mom and Hubert shared more than a love of our nation's civics; they both had cancer. Hubert was a principled liberal who kept fighting the good fight, Mom was a die-hard conservative who, even after the mastectomies and the chemo, mustered the strength to belt out a powerful rendition of 'The Lord's Prayer' at my sister Chell and Russ's wedding in August. I was 14 years old, in my first tuxedo, it was hot, and I passed out in front of God and everyone.

Within days of completing the civics project that fall, cancer began to play its cards and took Granddad Aleshire in October. They wouldn't let me see him to say goodbye. They said I should remember him as he was.

I didn't get a proper farewell but did get some 'me time' with Grandad the previous spring. A doctor diagnosed a recurring stomachache as a spastic colon. Mom's cure was to put me on a bus for Illinois to spend time with a grandfather I didn't know was dying.

For ten days I rode around with Grandad visiting sale barns and old-timey storytellers at grain elevators. We took long walks through the woods and lit controlled burns of brush piles while grandad told tales that, for some reason, were more philosophical than his usual lighthearted stories.

Grandad Howard, 'Pat' Aleshire, loved to imitate the accent of his brother-in-law, Frank Alexander, who turned his nickname, Pat, into 'Pot'. 'Uncle Fronk,' would say, "by God, Pot, whatta we gonna do now'?"

At Grandad's wake, I stood over a face I barely recognized and said, "By God, Pot, what am I gonna do now?" about ten times before being asked to let someone else have a turn at not recognizing the man who introduced us to a million characters, taught us how to work, whittle, judge livestock, ride horses, drive cars, shoot guns, and tell tales.

By Christmas break in '75, life was stumbling toward less than normal. My oldest sister, Chell, was married, number two, Rhonda moved to the farm to go to nursing school and help Gram. Three of us were teenagers and did our best to help with the Little Girls. Mom wasn't home one day when Missy, Andi, and I returned from sledding.

"Where's mom?" I asked Jenny, who was just old enough to get news reports.

"At the hospital," she replied.

"When's she comin' home?"

"She's not."

The restaurants and Grandad were gone, Mom was poised to join them, and the family farm was in decay. I walked into the bathroom and closed the door to cry but couldn't. I just stared at myself in the mirror asking the boy staring back what the hell was wrong with a kid who couldn't cry over the impending death of his mother.

When I got my private time to say goodbye to Mom at Eitel Hospital, I said nothing and sobbed uncontrollably til she couldn't take it anymore. Chell gently escorted me from the room. My ever-protective brother passed on a message of love from Mom and the slightly surprising news that she'd made peace with Jesus.

She died on Saturday, January 10th, 1976. I was at the old neighborhood rink on Upton Avenue playing hockey with the boys. When I saw my new brother-in-law's car pull up, I knew what day it was. He shared the news and asked if I wanted to go with him or stay. I stayed and asked myself what the hell kind of a kid plays hockey after the news of his mother's death.

There were two funerals. One in Bloomington at a funeral home up a hill and across the street from Nine Mile Creek; next door to the Presbyterian church where I was first baptized. We stayed in Illinois for a week after funeral number two and conducted a 19th century ritual of gathering in the front parlor of the farmhouse to reconcile mom's departure. Parlors (elegant living rooms) were once reserved for sacred family gatherings like weddings and funerals.

About 20 of us gathered, and the country preacher asked us to join hands in a circle of prayer. Jenny's shoulders started to bounce in an uncontrollable giggle that was more powerful than Pop's ominous stare as the giggle spread throughout the family and confounded the preacher. We couldn't help but think of the warning to "Be wary of God-fearin' Christians and circles of prayer." Mom wasn't physically with us that day, but owned the room one last time.

When I returned to my eighth-grade classes at Nicollet Jr. High School, only one teacher asked where I'd been for a week: my Spanish teacher, Senora Boroff. She said, "We missed you, Diego (my Spanish class name) have you been out of town?"

"Yes, at a funeral," I replied.

"Ohh, did you lose a grandparent?" she asked with a sympathetic smile.

"No, my mom."

I'll never forget how her smile turned to a look of anguish. She was obviously aghast that nobody informed her of the nature of my absence. It was the most sincere and touching moment of condolence I received in that time.

"I know," I said to answer the look on her face. "They keep everything a secret."

***

We weren't in the face-to-face apartments much longer. I was told when to pack, and Pop moved us closer to his roots in the western suburbs, to an old farmhouse – home number twelve – that was tucked into a neighborhood across the street from mini-mansions on the shores of Lake Minnetonka. Before going west, I visited my spot, but it didn't feel sacred. It didn't feel anything. I just stared at the dirt below the rock and didn't cry.

Life by the lake lasted less than a year, but we packed a lot into the months. It was the summer of the Bicentennial, and the nation took a brief, patriotic break from the disgraces of Vietnam and Nixon's Watergate scandal that forever altered our collective self-esteem; and when Viking I landed on Mars, it foreshadowed a day when perhaps the world would not fight forever over oil.

President Gerald Ford was like an uncle everyone seemed to trust, and he had the nation trending in the right direction, but he leap-frogged into the presidency by appointment, and when the elections rolled around in November, the nation chose a humble and charismatic idealist named Jimmy Carter to do his best to set a new course for our country. The political machines devoured his intentions and we all slipped further into division and self-loathing.

The Burnsville boys buoyed my spirits that summer with trips to the lake. They took half-day city bus rides to come hang out with me. We'd meet in downtown Minneapolis to ride our skateboards at the Federal Reserve Bank Plaza with its half-a-square-block of concrete at a 15-degree tilt that made it a skateboarding mecca.

We'd hop on the #15 bus out to a little lake town called Navarre, then walk a mile to our house and suit up to splash houseboat owners with 'can-openers' and 'cannonballs' by jumping into channels from highway and railroad bridges. We'd take canoes out to a bay called 'cruiser country' to purposely fight the waves in a contest to see who could last longest without getting swamped.

The second love-of-my-life, Annie, even made the trek out from Burnsville. She, like Ginger in Illinois, would be always 'a friend.'

I didn't have any 'buddies' at the new lakeside school but made comfortable acquaintances in the last days of eighth grade; the cool kids viewed me as an enigma and didn't totally ignore me. On my first day in Phys-ed, I hit a homerun while wearing corduroys and a short-sleeved dress shirt. The pants were ruined, and Pop just nodded as if to say, 'I would have slid, too.'

About three days into my classes at Minnetonka West the next fall, an overzealous English teacher had us reading awkward, medieval poetry aloud to each other. She called on me.

"Let's have our new student read. Michael, would you honor us with your rendition of the next verse?" she invited, with a theatrical lilt reserved for Jr. High English teachers and Renaissance Festival performers.

I looked down at the line from 'The Second Shepherd's Play': *Woe is my cock, for he is in the shackles*, then looked up with my beet-red face and said, "No. Way."

The girl next to me scrunched her beet-red face and nodded to silently thank me on behalf of the whole 9th grade class.

Life on – well, near – the lake was a dramatic departure from the south-suburban house-hopping of the previous few years. My buddies and I were expatriates like Hemingway's gang - in a domestic, 15-year-old kind of way. The adventures absorbed my pain, for a while.

***

In '76, brother Ringo turned 18 and declared his independence. I lost my hand-me-down benefactor who set off like a secret agent. Nobody heard from him for a year and a half, til he showed up one day, opened the fridge, sighed and said, "There's no milk."

I wasn't the only kid still at home in '76, and Pop decided the best way to minimize disruption was to take the remaining four back to familiar friends and families in Burnsville. He got a great deal from a local legend named Jack Young who rented us lucky home #13, back in the Knob Hill neighborhood where we had rented for a while after the house fire. It was less than a mile from my favorite high ground.

There was, however, an anomaly. The house was in Burnsville, but due to an ancient and incongruous school district boundary, this house at the dead-end of Aldrich Avenue was the only one on the block that was in Rosemount-Apple Valley School District #196.

Appeals to bureaucrats were futile. I was off to the tenth of eleven schools of my childhood.

Apple Valley High was brand new in 1976. Demographics and suburban sprawl made it the crème-de-la-crème of metro high schools. District 196 was well-funded, and well-run. There would be no five-year plan. Apple Valley would succeed early and often in the late '70s – without any help from me.

Above-average athletic ability was always my route to integration in school-to-school life. I'd patiently wait, then make a nice play, and get accepted into a new tribe. It happened in Bloomington, twice in Macomb, in Lima, Minnetonka, and three times in Burnsville. It didn't happen in Apple Valley. Not once.

I played listless and shy, and below average on the football team. I thought about quitting – a concept that is weak and treasonous in our family.

Pop tried to rally me with a pep-talk. He knew my passion for Civil War history and delivered a brilliant correlation about how this point in my life was like a personal Gettysburg, a critical moment where decisions and reactions would define the years to come. The epic address fell on spiteful ears. How could he know that his 15-year-old, high school sophomore-of-a-son was a Rebel sympathizer who still thought States Rights were more important than human dignity? I never told him I was still pissed at General Lee for making the name 'Pickett' synonymous with ignominious defeat.

'To hell with football practice,' I thought one day in September of '76. I walked out of an Apple Valley classroom and eyeballed an emergency exit with no alarm. This was an emergency. I had to get away. I set my spiral notebook on the well-waxed floor and knelt to tie my shoe. I glanced left-right-left after the hallway cleared of kids I didn't know, then headed for the door. After a simple palm-shove of the bar, I stepped outside and listened to a spring-loaded wedge of stainless-steel clack behind to declare me free and clear – and truant.

My plan was to slip out the north door, slide into the neighborhood, then slink off to the school of my pals, Burnsville High, the home of the Braves. Once outside, I stepped away from the glass door, pressed against the brick wall, and adjusted my internal compass to true north. It pointed at hundreds of yards of lush, green athletic fields that suddenly looked like San Francisco Bay to an Alcatraz inmate. I turned back and tried the door, but the stainless-steel wedge had become a euphemism for life's decisions.

I had a decent 40-yard dash time as a kid, but this looked like a mile of wide-open prairie. The school's snipers would have plenty of time to pick me off. With nothing to lose, I decided instead to play it cool and began to walk with purpose and the ready-made excuse of a doctor's appointment. The march to liberty began on soft, well-mowed, Kentucky Bluegrass as I paraded like a 1st Virginian at Gettysburg over the open field. I kept marching, but no shots or shouts ever came. Nobody cared.

The four miles of terrain between the lowlands of Apple Valley and the bluffs of Burnsville was a ponderous climb, like the rise of Pennsylvania's Cemetery Ridge. I made the self-righteous march with no consideration of consequence – until one presented itself.

A stop at my sacred spot had not been pre-meditated. It happened upon me, like suddenly running into an old friend. It was 65 degrees on the way to 80 at 9:30 a.m. that day. A gentle, southwest wind carried puffy clouds from Edina to Minneapolis, then over the Cathedral of St. Paul.

I reached the crest to survey the horizon as tears dripped from my cheeks. My shoulders leaned back and dragged down the tree til I sat upon the big round rock. A muddled reflection was squarely rooted between pubescence and manhood.

When the tears stopped, I sat up straight and stared at the horizon like a king in exile. My naïve reign over a 302-acre empire at the farm had gone the way of the Habsburgs and Byzantines. Forts of Lincoln Logs and Erector Sets were abandoned, my vast army of plastic men was discharged, and the undefeated navy of horse troughs and six-panel doors that once ruled the waters was decommissioned. Motel chair-thrones were removed from the wrap-around porch of my castle, and all flights on a tire swing from a huge, regal maple were cancelled.

I knew no one at the new school. I liked nothing. I had no farm life to look forward to, and no mother to remind me how strong I could be when things got tough. Family values might have mattered, if I had given them a thought, if the lessons hadn't been overwhelmed by the selfish uncertainty of teenaged neurology.

My surrogate-mother/sisters set off on new journeys that didn't include a little towhead who'd turned into a treasonous teen. The big brother who dragged me along on countless adventures finally found a way to ditch me, and I felt like a horse-drawn manure spreader abandoned in a ravine.

I stared, then started to pick out triggering landmarks. One of mom's sayings came to mind: "Michael," she'd say, "it's not how big, or strong, or fast you are; it's how tough you can get." She was still with me. I couldn't quit, that would be treasonous.

In 1976, the horizon from the sacred spot was endless as always. I looked at St. Paul, Minneapolis, Edina then Bloomington to remember explorations with Jimmy Brinkhaus. I went north again and thought of Grandpa Pickett who got blown up in The Great War but lived on without the ability to see puffy clouds and horizons.

I still had grandmas, Eula Jaunita and Beulah Cornelia. They'd prob'ly never die.

I thought about the football practice I was about to skip and felt guilty and weak.

We moved again before the end of September 1976. Home number fourteen would be deeper into District 196 and send me to number eleven of the eleven schools of my youth: Rosemount High.

Our new home was a desperate place at first, with a refrigerator that had only a bottle of mustard and an egg at times. We, like our neighbors, were subsidized, but not for long. Pop rallied. He designed and managed the food service facility that fed the largest medical center in the region. He didn't have much time for me, but he did his best, and that was good enough.

Shirley and Don Lusk and their son Dan adopted me part-time - as had Gladys and Bob and Bruce Michelsen in Burnsville – to reinforce examples of how important stability and consistency is to a young mind.

The small-town and farm kids of Rosemount were welcoming and felt familiar. By 1979, they had restored my royal status – if only as a prince and for only one night in a homecoming court. I guess I made a nice play somewhere along the line – I know Dan Lusk did. The kids gave us captains' stars for our football letter jackets and became a forever part of an extended family. They planted a perennial seed of reminder in me, that when a willing spirit is sprinkled with love, the universe is filled with infinite horizons.

Part Eleven

'THE LIST'

In October of 1980, 72 young men were competing for 48 seats on a jet airliner that would fly the Augsburg College football team from Minneapolis/St. Paul's Wold-Chamberlain Field to Denver's Stapleton – the old airport, not their new one that's half-way back to Minnesota.

The 48 winners would dress in blue sport coats – the coaches in Auggie maroon – and fly off to the Mile High City, then site-see their way down to Colorado Springs to face the Tigers of Colorado College. During the tour of duty and purpose, the Auggies would parade with the disciplined cadets of the Air Force Academy, ascend to the heights of Pike's Peak, and commune at the scenic Garden of the Gods.

I was one of the 72 competitors, and far from a star, but a sure-fire bet to be on that plane. The roster had me on every special team and I'd traveled to every away game for the Division III football team, including the school's biggest win in 50 years – a 21-10 victory at the homecoming of powerhouse St. John's University.

I was the wedge buster on the kick-off squad; one who sacrificed his body – sideways if necessary – to occupy as many of the three blockers as possible when they set up to protect the return man. On the kick and punt return teams, I was semi-deep and one of two guys who would try to pick off the opposing wedge buster.

On the punt-block team, I was the outside guy who sprinted toward the point of the kicker's release – and once again sacrifice my body in a desperate, diving attempt to block the punt, as Scott Severson, a really tall guy, went simultaneously up the middle with the same objective.

Posting of the Colorado Springs travel roster after Tuesday's practice would make it official: 'Sever' and I would be going after some mile-high punts.

Blue sport coats were required, so the chosen 48 could project a unified image of respect and character. We were young men venturing off to a foreign land in defense of the virtue of our Institution and home state. Jerry Rezac didn't have a jacket, but I had two. I loaned him one and most certainly would be wearing the other, the question was how much playing time I'd get.

In addition to being a main stay on the special teams, I was #2 on the depth chart at my defensive back position. The rank was a bit dubious, however, in that I was behind an All-Conference guy named Bob Dorgan who was 3 inches taller, two steps faster, could jump higher, and grow a one-day beard that would take me a semester. But even all-conference guys need rest, so I was hopeful.

Augsburg, a small, frugal institution of austere Lutheran heritage at the time, rarely broke into the piggy bank for such exotic travel, so flying in an airplane to an outstate contest gave us humble sons of stoic faith a tiny taste of Big-Time athletics. Making the travel roster was a huge deal, but nary a worry for me. I didn't even bother to check 'The List.'

My buddy and eventual best man, Mike "Chief" Weidner, however, was on the bubble. The 8.5x11 piece of copy paper was hand-typed through ribbons of ink and carried into the locker room by an assistant trainer who usually dragged bags of stinky laundry. On this fateful Tuesday evening, he carried the writ with divine purpose and posted it – like Martin Luther nailing up the Protestant treatise at Wittenberg – with a piece of white sports tape on a brick wall.

After practice, bubble guys like Chief would gather their courage and mosey over one at a time to take a hopeful peek. He returned with a scrunched-up face and shaking his head.

"Didn't make it, huh?" I said with consoling disappointment. I was gonna miss having him on the trip.

"No," he said, "didn't think I would, but that ain't it."

"What ain't what?"

"Uh… Pic… you ain't on the list either."

I laughed. Chief and I would eventually be the team's unofficial 'hazing' captains (not crazy Ivy League rituals, just ridiculous, spontaneous pranks on freshmen) so his gag was transparently lame.

"Yeah, right," I scoffed, but he kept it up and was either doing his best acting ever or being sincere.

"Sorry, man, but I'm not kiddin' – go check it out."

I gave him an 'OK, I'll bite' look and walked toward the treatise – now only half as confident as a moment before.

'The List' was alphabetical: Nayman, Quam, Rezac, Roff. Wait a second… Nayman, Quam, Rezac, Roff… Nayman, Quam, Rezac, Roff. No Pickett. No Pickett. No Pickett.

I processed four of the five stages of mourning – denial, anger, bargaining, depression – within a minute: There must be a mistake. How the hell does so-and-so get to go but not me? I'll go talk to Ozzie, he'll set it straight. What if he doesn't? I was angry, sad, confused, and embarrassed – there was no Stage Five, no acceptance. The bubble guys who'd seen 'The List,' and probably also thought I was going, just looked into their lockers as I passed.

Chief did his best to console me. "Hey, man, look at the bright side. We'll have a few days off and there'll be less competition for women."

It didn't work. I was already wondering how I'd break the news to Pop and the family, and to my co-workers at the publishing company where I was a popular assistant mail clerk who was living a college lifestyle worthy of their imaginations.

I didn't have to go bargain with Ozzie, coach Jack Osberg; he sought me out.

"Picker," as he called me, "c'mere. I need to talk to you."

Jack Osberg is a player's coach, and a coach's coach. He's a man's, a woman's, and a child's man. He's gracious, full of faith, and humble to purpose. He can be tough as a kidney stone as a competitor, soft as cream cheese in a kolache as a husband, friend, dad, or grandpa. Ozzie has a frequent, unbalanced sort of smile that he constantly talks through, and uses to express a plethora of emotions – from joy and candor, to warning.

He's a field general and a social worker who is perpetually positive and even after turning 80, the former high school science teacher still coaches and remains idol and mentor to hundreds. The only time I broke down at my father's memorial service in 2013, was when Jack and his equally inspiring wife, Nina, walked through the door.

He needed to talk to me about Ward Miller.

Our football team, like most Division III (D3) teams, was loaded with tough characters who could be gentlemen, and the meanest bastards you ever met on a field of competition. D3 athletes are among the best in their high school conferences, but 98% of us don't possess quite enough size, or speed, or skill to earn scholarships at the big-time schools.

Ward Miller fit in to the gentleman category. He wasn't particularly fast or strong, and certainly not mean. He was studious, polite, and reliable as rain. He never missed a practice in four years, and never cracked a starting lineup. He was the consummate practice player and invaluable to the team's success.

Ozzie explained Ward Miller to me and said that's why they were taking him, rather than me, to Colorado.

"This trip is more than a football game, Picker," he said. "It's an extension of the collegiate experience and an opportunity to thank seniors for their sacrifice and commitment. Your time will come."

I couldn't help but understand. A trip on an airplane to play a football game was too good to be true, anyway. I felt like I blocked a punt then got called for being offsides. The acceptance of Stage Five in the mourning process began to creep into my heart but left plenty of room for a selfish pout.

The next day at a no-pads, dry-run practice, the coaches called out the kick-off team for a simulation of responsibilities. Ten guys ran onto the field.

"Cripes all Friday! That's ten! Where the hell is our wedge man?" Head coach Al Kloppen hollered. "Jesus... let's go, Pickett!"

Seventy-two players and eight coaches went silent. The heads turned to me...

"I'm not on the travel roster!" I shouted back with part explanation, part accusation.

I agreed with the coaches' decision and was even happy for Ward, but the moment had a sting of rubbed-in public embarrassment.

Coach Al paused, gathered himself, then muttered, "Oh... uh, yeah... Bobby, jump in there. Let's go!"

There's no way you'd put a lanky, all-conference safety known for savvy finesse – like Bob Dorgan – into that reckless role of human sacrifice, but Al did some quick thinking and picked a name he knew was on 'The List' to move beyond the unpleasant pause as quickly as possible.

My locker was front and center in the locker room. I sat on a metal folding chair and began to peel off athletic socks, and some of the disappointment as I felt unstated empathy from Colorado travelers, bubble guys, and no-chance Freshmen alike. One of the team's best smart-asses, top locker-room personalities, and a starting offensive tackle, Dean Hattenburger, completely broke the ice as he walked past.

"Well! That was fucking awkward!" he belted out for all to hear, then rubbed my head like he was Wally and I the Beaver. "Cheer up, Pic. You'll live."

His reference to the 800-pound gorilla in the room further lightened the mood. Guys chuckled and whatever compassion was in the room helped me inch closer to full acceptance.

As we dressed and straggled out of the locker room, Ozzie approached me again.

"Picker, I need to talk..."

I cut him off with closed eyes and a shake of my head. "It's OK, coach. I'm all right. Everything's good."

Ozzie put his hands on my shoulders. "No. I need to talk to you," he said through a "good news" version of that smile.

"Picker, you're going to Colorado," Ozzie said. "Round up a blue sports coat and be here at 5:45 tomorrow morning. Nelly (trainer Doug Nelson) is packing your gear."

Departure was less than 12 hours away. I was stunned.

I was still processing acceptance. "What?"

"Sever," Ozzie said. "He's injured and can't play."

My would-be punt-blocking partner, Scott Severson, played high school ball at Northfield, MN in the same conference as me; "The Mighty Missota." Unlike Hattenburger, guys like Sever were low-key types who piped in occasionally with one-liners. He was eminently likeable, and his notoriously mellow demeanor disguised a deeper quality previously unknown to me.

I was horrified that they pulled him from 'The List.'

"Yeah, but he's a Senior, he should still get to go," I begged.

Jack explained, "Scott came into the coaches' office and said, 'no way I'm gonna go stand on the sidelines in street clothes while Pic is sitting here at home. Send him in my place.'"

Not dead yet. Add another emotion. I was overwhelmed and wanted to cheer and leap to throw my fist in the air but a sense of guilt and unworthiness crept into my heart.

"No. No. No." I said. "Sever deserves to go. He can't do that. I can't." I was saying words I had to say – and deep down believed – but deeper down, didn't want to. "Sever can't do that," I repeated.

"He did, and it's done," Jack said. "Put on a blue coat and be on that bus." By now he was talking through a new smile; this one expressed pride in the character of one young man, and joy for the opportunity it transferred to another.

The next morning at six a.m., a motorcoach idled outside the 1960s Bauhaus bricks of Sigurd Melby Athletic Hall on the Augsburg campus. The building was dedicated on the day I was born and, obviously, was a pre-destined point of departure. The bus was full of proud young men in blue sport coats, including the one I loaned Jerry Rezac. At 6:08, it departed for MSP International Airport… without Scott Severson, and without me.

The alarm on my plastic desk clock wasn't set to ring for another 11 hours and 12 minutes, at 5 o'clock p.m. on October 16, 1980. It was a simple oversight, an easily understood sophomore mistake. Senior Ward Miller was on time and on board, as he had been 500 times in a row.

My mind was instantly suspicious when the eyes opened without an alarm. It's amazing how many thoughts and emotions a human brain can process in less than a second. Why did I wake up without an alarm? What day is it? What time? This is the biggest day of my life. Please tell me it's 4:50 in the morning…

It was 5:48 and I lived off campus, at least 20 minutes west of Mr. Melby's Hall.

Smiling Jack flashed in my mind, with yet another variation; a confounded look accompanied by a boom of his signature question when young men were making simple oversights: "What in the Sam Hill is goin' on here!?"

I trembled with fears of his disappointment, of reducing Sever's selfless act to dust, of missing the greatest experience a second-rate, small-time athlete could ever expect. I was dead in the water but couldn't give up. I pulled on the blue coat then paused at my dresser long enough to run a checklist through my head. Keys-Wallet-ID-toothbrush. Go! Travelling was less complicated in 1980.

It's also amazing how strategic a human brain can become in the midst of panic. I grabbed my bag of clothes and sprinted out the door:

I'll go to Si Melby just in case they were setting us up and the bus wasn't leaving til 6:30. If it's not there, I'll peel out to the airport with one of those short-cuts the South Minneapolis guys showed me. I'll park the car then figure out how to pay for it later. If the plane hasn't left, I'd throw myself at Ozzie's feet and beg for merciful forgiveness of this heinous, irresponsible, disrespectful act. I'll offer up a false promise to never again screw up a once-in-a-lifetime opportunity.

A duffle bag thumped my back with each stride of a sprint through the parking garage and up the steps, two, sometimes three, at a time. I emerged into the cavernous terminal to people scurrying like ants into long lines that led to airline agents staring at screens and typing in endless sequence.

I begged a uniformed airport employee where I might find the Augsburg football team.

"What? Where they going?" the man asked back.

"Colorado," I pleaded, "We're going to play a football game at Colora..."

"Bunch of college kids in blue blazers?" he interrupted.

"Yes! Yes!"

"They left," he said.

Oh, shit.

He pointed through large plate glass windows.

The team and coaches were loitering at drop-off, outside the terminal. It was two hours to lift-off and the ominous six a.m. deadline had morphed into a listless crowd of bored young men in uncomfortable clothes awaiting adventure.

I was relieved and thankful, but still had to make things right with a humble plea to Coach Osberg. He saw me swimming through the blue coats, and gave another iteration of a mentor's smile as he shook his head; this one was welcoming and implied: "You don't do anything the easy way, do you?"

"Hey, Picker! Good to see you. I knew you'd figure it out."

I'd won the sure-fire bet and made 'The List' after all. I lived the trip that ended up being great, but more epic in memory than it was in real time.

The respectful young men of character dutifully endured a three-hour cog railway ride up and down a mountain. One of us tried to commandeer a souvenir jersey from the Air Force Academy's locker room, and we all passed anonymously through a closed room til it reappeared. We chanted "No Garden of the Gods" together, til the coaches gave up on the tour to let us go play cards or wander the heights of Colorado Springs.

The 48 played well on a perfect, sunny day at a beautiful, mountaintop stadium to defeat the Tigers 27-10, and I had the first tackle of the game by dodging the wedge altogether and nailing the return man at the 12-yard line. They moved Ward Miller up to #2 for the day and he got some long-awaited playing time.

Jack Osberg walked the sidelines as time expired with a smile that quantified Miller's ends, justified Severson's means, and reminded me that all's well that ends well – and, with faith – all ends well.

Part Twelve

JUST IN TIME

Time – it's one of the great forces of the universe; but it doesn't really exist, it just happens. It's endless, and fleeting. We want it to speed up, then slow down. We try to capture it in snapshots of how we used to look, and how it used to feel. We measure it, waste it, try to kill – then save it; but no matter what we do, it keeps slipping away.

I ran in to Dennis Czech at 179 Snelling Avenue – Macalester College stadium – in St. Paul on September 26, 1981. He was a running back for Mac, I played defensive back for Augsburg College. Each of us was attempting to persuade time to be on our side.

Morning clouds drizzled droplets then thinned by game time to let sun and shade take turns on the field of competition til it was a perfect combination of warm and cool, soft and firm. The game kicked off at 61 degrees, and drifting cumulus affirmed long-sleeves for student spirit-wear. An ideal football Saturday had arrived in autumnal equinox.

Dennis Czech used perfect timing more than once that afternoon. On one particular play he made a cut that freed him into the defensive secondary where he became my responsibility.

I had been waiting three years for the obligation. I wanted to run into Czech, or someone like him, and tackle him to the ground. Dennis was an all-state player at Cretin High School in 1978, our senior high school season, and by '81 was among the best in our collegiate league. I was a two-time honorable mention also-ran to our high school All-Conference team and hoping patience and practice had prepared me to be a competitive NCAA Division III football player. Defensive coordinator, Jack Osberg, sensed the time was right and had me in the starting lineup.

I had to wait three years for a chance to tackle a guy like Dennis Czech because the timing belt that connected my brain and limbs had gone out of sync. The belt had been greased by doubt and uncertainty to make synapses spit out confusing messages that had my arms and legs zagging when they should have been zigging. This was contrary to a lifetime of recreation where wrangling over strips of sod and gravel with my pals was done with reckless, automatic joy.

The youthful bliss returned on September 26, 1981. I was back in sync. Reading keys, taking on lead blockers, and tackling an all-state running back came with clear confidence and made the game even more fun than out-running Jimmy Brinkhaus on a childhood sandlot. The payoff from practice and patience was delightful. I knew I belonged and was having the time of my life.

Dennis Czech zigged when he needed to, then zagged into a sprint with about a minute remaining in the first half. He was faster and quicker, but the geometry of football pursuit-angles was once again intuitive to my synapses. I knew he'd try to beat me around the corner, then lower his shoulder for an attempt at an extra yard when he ran out of space and time.

One prefers to hit rather than be hit, so as we neared the sideline, I went low and wrapped my arm around his lower back as I drove my left shoulder pad into his rib cage and my helmet in front of his torso. Czech was dangerous as a loose timing belt, so I was taking no chances as I corralled him near midfield after a gain of three or four yards – about half the distance of the slippery St. Paulite's average run.

We weren't the only two players on the field however, and my teammate, Jesse Quam, wanted to tackle Dennis Czech as well. Quam was an all-stater too, one of the largest players in the league, and the beast was only a split-second behind me in forty-yard dash time.

As I stalked and strung the runner out toward the sidelines, Jesse closed the gap from midfield in a full sprint; he engulfed both me and Dennis as the three of us crashed to the turf in front of our bench where we were met with a hail of cheers and atta-boy helmet slaps from our teammates and coaches.

Czech scrambled out of the pile and ran back to his huddle; Jesse did the same.

I remained; a biproduct of a violent game.

After slowly rolling to the right, I pushed myself up with the arm that still functioned. My left shoulder socket was propped over Czech's mid-section as the full force of a Quam-ton thundered upon us. The snap, crackle, and pop of the landing was muffled by the exuberance of our teammates.

I staggered to my feet and pushed through a crowd of players and butt slaps that were the congratulatory mode of the day, to find the athletic trainer and let him know the pain in the dangling left arm would soon pass. "It's just a pinch, Nelly. Happened all the time in high school." I said in eager anticipation of continuing my meetings with Czech.

Doug Nelson would soon know better. "Just stand still," he said as he groped under my pads. "Hmm... uhh, no... this isn't a pinched nerve, Pickett. It's all the way out."

"Whatta ya mean," I said between winces.

"Your shoulder is completely out of the socket. You're going to the hospital."

"Whatta ya mean?" I said in further denial. "I can't play anymore?"

"Not today."

"What? When?"

"...Who knows..." he added, then yelled to his assistant, "Jane! Get me the radio."

Time had expired. They eased me out of my pads and into a sling. As Nelly walkie-talkie squawked to nearby Midway hospital, I trundled over to defensive coordinator Osberg.

"Hey, Ozzie. Don't make me go. Let me stick around for the win."

We were ahead by a couple of scores, and I wanted to savor the victory. I wanted to shake Czech's hand and let him know I'd see him again. I didn't want to part with the uniqueness of a moment in time where the joy of youthful instinct, patient practice, and the ambition to prove I belonged had arrived in equinox.

"Nelly thinks it's pretty serious, Picker. You better go." Ozzie said through one side of his mouth.

"Oh, mannn," I whined more desperately, "c'monnn, coach... I might be out for a while and really wanna stay for this one. Pleeeze?"

Ozzie gave the trainer a questioning look, Nelly shrugged and said, "if you can take the pain, it's up to you. Maybe it'll pop back in... if it does, you're sure gonna know it."

I stuck around, and it didn't pop back in, but I sure knew it was there. The contorted ligaments and broken socket began to ache a bit more with each point the Macalester Scots scored during a second-half comeback. I ambled with a throbbing helplessness past teammates to sit on an empty bench. They responded like farm kids and would pass by, silently pat me on the head, then leave me on the porch like an old hound who they loved but who had seen his last hunt.

Time expired again in the 2nd and final half with Dennis Czech in our end zone – my end zone – for their first conference win in a decade. I would have saved the game, my heart insisted, if not for a broken socket. I would have tackled that all-stater just in time. I had rediscovered the confident joy of play; my brain and body – even the weather – was in sync.

But the limb was limp, my football moment had slipped away, and he kept right on zigging and zagging with perfect timing.

I ran in to Dennis Czech at 550 Albert Street in St. Paul – a multi-purpose, artificial turf athletic complex named Wingerd Field on the campus of his alma mater, Cretin-Derham Hall high school. He was a high school girls softball coach; I was the public address announcer. It was a cool April afternoon 40 years after our first meeting.

Czech started popping up in my neighborhood 25 years earlier – or, since he'd lived there his whole life – I guess it was me who popped in. We had met a couple dozen times by that day – at church Men's Club events, coaching our daughters' youth teams, at Mancini's Restaurant, some volunteer gig, or as he and his wife Sheila took daily walks through the neighborhood.

Dennis Czech and I aren't close buddies, I mean, I wouldn't call him to help me move a heavy couch or replace a water heater. He's one of those people I'm allowed to take for granted, and he, me. We're like time capsules of each other's lives that we get to open on random occasions. Each and every time, we both automatically smile at the sight of each other, have a pleasant chat that never includes promises to get together more often, then sign off with a re-affirming smile and handshake… til next time.

I've peeked at the rear-view mirror where time reveals itself as the great teacher of all things and healer of all wounds. My play time on a football field was not cut short. I saw, and breathed, and felt equinox in my synapses, in my pours, in temperature and barometric pressure. I felt it in a sense of achievement and belonging. I felt it in my shoulder and, eventually, in my soul.

At halftime on September 26, 1981, 'life and time' gave me a lesson that only dramatic change – often accompanied by pain – can deliver. If the injury had arrived two hours, a day, a week, or a year before, it might have been too early, but it waited til I got to experience the delightful joy of running into an all-stater like Dennis Czech.

It all happened, just in time.

PART THIRTEEN

SCHOOL IS OUT

As Ralph Waldo Emerson said, "The years teach much that the days never know."

In the late 1980s, I dabbled in the business of Big Education with a three-quarter time job in a para-professional gig at St. Paul's Highland Park High School. I'd been coaching football for a couple of years and really enjoyed the kids. Career positions were scarce – unemployment was about ten percent – so I also did freelance creative work and supplemented my portfolio as a bartender and umpire; or, to cite one of Pop's lectures, I lacked "specific intent."

St. Paul had established a Post-Secondary Resource Center in each high school library to support overworked guidance counsellors, and I was toying with the idea of challenging my lack of intent with a return to college for a teaching certificate when I interviewed for a position as manager of the Highland Park Resource Center.

America's public schools were once our greatest asset and institution. Back in 19th century Massachusetts, Horace Mann envisioned a model that would become a philosophical and functional extension of both our Declaration of Independence and the Constitution. One historian said of Mann:

"No one did more than he to establish in the minds of the American people the conception that education should be universal, non-sectarian, free, and that its aims should be social efficiency, civic virtue, and character, rather than mere learning or the advancement of sectarian ends."

Americans held on to, perpetuated, and innovated those principles for about a hundred years. By the turn of the 20th century, however, the responsibility to educate our young turned into an industry. Social efficiency and civic virtue gave way to unchecked budgets and ever-widening achievement gaps. Somewhere around 1980, the check and balance of Parent-Teacher Associations disappeared behind a curtain of administrators and union officials.

I was offered the job and, times being what they were, I accepted, and retained the opportunity to work with the kids. In between incredibly stupid actions and life choices, they'd show flashes of maturity, brilliance, and promise. I could relate to them. As it turned out, they taught me far more than whatever I left behind in that library.

As one might imagine, work behind the scenes at a school exposes one to a cross-section of America. Lots of average people, some lazy, some angry and selfish. The administration is too powerful and wasteful, the parents are too detached or too defensive, and teachers have been stripped of any authority in their classrooms.

Our schools, however, still have the distinction of employing the most exceptional, selfless people in the nation for the lowest compensation. Thousands of brilliant minds take their bonuses through amortized joy that may not arrive until they accidentally run into a thankful student 20 years after graduation.

The kids make it worthwhile. They inspire and break hearts on a daily basis. That's why I didn't become a teacher. I was too emotional to leave it at school. I needed to save every kid, solve every problem, and celebrate every success, with every kid. This wasn't gonna happen. My passion for the daily interaction caught the cancer and I drifted away to leave the career to one better suited; and Mrs. Levine was.

I had a fraction of the experiences that real teachers get but retain fond memories of unique and fascinating personalities. One, actually two, of my favorites were a pair of girls who thought like identical twins and looked like the number ten. Livvy was tall and pencil thin, Nettie was short and round. They were self-confident beyond their years and dished out wisdom like a serious version of Laurel and Hardy.

St. Paul's Lutheran activists were helping Hmong and Southeast Asian families re-establish in St. Paul and I met Cheng, who was going to become a famous writer and tell the world of his family's arduous journey. Another young man couldn't wait to join the military, then return to his homeland in a jet fighter to repay Pol Pot and the Khmer Rouge for their atrocities.

I worked with a gifted football player who tried to cheat on his ACT to qualify for an NCAA scholarship. He was humbled when he got caught, but still perplexed as to why a couple of wrong answers on a stupid test could keep him from playing college football.

There was at least one 17-year-old girl who lived alone in an apartment and supported herself.

The Highland Park and Macalester/Groveland neighborhoods in St. Paul are a national anomaly. The income demographics are a blend of old money, upper middle class, paycheck-to-paycheck wannabes, and lunch bucket grinders who are good with their money. It's an urban blend of small-town and suburbia made up of 89% white people who live just ten minutes from an international airport and two major cities.

An '80s bussing program turned the hallways of Highland Park High School into a demographic kaleidoscope. In addition to the newly arriving southeast Asians, there were Black, Brown, and Indian students. There were probably Indigenous Americans too, but nobody gave them a thought. Being Gay wasn't yet accepted as an overt inclination, but most of the kids were aware. This was just before people courageously started 'coming out' and back when gender identity was a scientific fact, rather than a political agenda item.

My favorite group of kids at school was the bowling team. I was their coach even though my benchmark for personal success was a hundred pins. The team needed an adult supervisor to be viable, and the captains approached me at my post in the library. I promised I couldn't add to their skills, but they said they just needed a live body and that the pay per hour was almost three times my usual hourly rate.

"I'm in," I said.

It was an eye-opener. These geeky kids were different – but then again, the same – as the football jocks I was used to coaching. The difference came in what the bowlers were intense about, the sameness in their net behavior.

Our fan base was smaller than the chess team's and I never met a single parent or guardian, but the competitors seemed to prefer it that way. The invitation to coach a tiny, urban high school club team wasn't exactly the president of Alabama reaching out to Nick Saban, but Nick and I shared the responsibility to toss in a life lesson here and there.

Highland was also home to the district's hearing-impaired program, and there were two kids of that unique culture, Sara and Dee, on the team. During a match at the old SkyLane Bowling Center in Minneapolis I started a sign language cheer for Dee by forming the letter 'D' with my fingers and thrusting it in a silent chant.

The American Sign Language 'D' forms a convenient "You're #1" shape as well. Contrary to common misconception, people who are considered 'Deaf' have hearing impairments of vastly varied degrees. Most have some sense of hearing and almost all can feel the vibrations of sound, so Dee could sense verbal encouragement, but the chant was too fun to pass up.

The skilled bowlers who actually ran the team – and once hissed at me for mandating participation of all team members – happily joined in what became a key bonding moment for the club.

I had a student aide for each classroom hour of the day. Getting to know their personal lives eventually led to the moments of pain that ended my teaching quest. I saw the incredible juxtaposition of lifestyles that came to work beside me five days a week and tried to chalk it up to a personal "that's life" pathos… until one day.

Rachel, a senior and my fourth hour aide, was a gregarious girl of Jewish descent whose father was a high-profile executive, and whose family lived in a large home not far from school.

Her eyes were red and puffy one Thursday – a condition that could mean a number of things in a high school kid. She had been crying, and as soon as I asked if she needed help with something, she started again. Her father had grounded her - just because he was stupid. And just because she happened to roll in at midnight on a Tuesday.

Rather than take her medicine, Rachel rebelled, and the method of her rebellion was guaranteed to exacerbate the situation.

"I was so mad at him, I took his credit card to the mall yesterday and spent $500," she said in a "so, there" tone.

I instantly thought of the '71 Chevy truck with ample rust that I had recently purchased for $350 and figured for $500, I could have bought one with a spare tire.

Rachel's sad frustration turned to self-righteous anger. "Ten o'clock, midnight, what's the big deal?" she asked, then continued. "I shouldn't have been grounded in the first place, so this is all his fault."

She bounced around with justifications before asking if I had any ideas. She was in pain, the most common kind, self-inflicted. Rachel knew she had doubled down in stupidity and was in a desperate search for a way out.

I remember thinking of how money complicated - but couldn't ease her pain - and sensed that even more than the actual punishment, she feared the inevitable pain of her father's disappointment. Her anxiety was so great that Rachel slept only an hour the night before. She said she couldn't eat.

I told her she had to fess up, but that flew over her head, so I tried to lighten her spirit, "Well, they're serving that nasty meat and brown water over fake potatoes today, anyway." I said.

She coughed out a slight laugh before leaving to join a friend and retell her woes.

Aaron, a sophomore, was my fifth hour aide. He wasn't big but was stout and had a personality that varied between sweet, tough, and staunchly determined. The dark-skinned young man took a city bus to get to Highland Park. He and his mother lived in an apartment across town. His father had no profile.

Aaron was especially quiet that day and had the look of someone who had lost something and was racking their brain to remember where it was. When I asked him to re-alphabetize a cart of college catalogs, he just nodded and went to work rather than fire off his usual million questions.

I was sitting at my desk doing paperwork and noticed that Aaron turned to look at me several times - as if to finally start his inquisition, but it never happened. Whenever I'd raise my eyebrows to silently ask "What's up?" he'd turn back to sorting books.

As the hour came to an end, Aaron stepped up and stood before me like a confessional kid who needed detention. I raised my eyebrows again.

"Hey, uh, Mike. Do you think you could loan me a dollar for lunch? Mom had to leave early this morning and must have forgotten to leave out my lunch money."

His mother didn't forget. I knew he paid for his own lunches. He was broke, and hungry for a plate of that nasty, fake starch.

I did my best to mask the $499 gut punch, and even though I had only four bucks – and my lunch cost two – I suddenly didn't care about the lack of a spare tire for my old truck.

"No problem," I said. He looked down as I handed him the dollar, I turned to a file cabinet behind me. We both were too proud to look the other in the eyes.

Mine were tearing up, but I couldn't let him see. He deserved to not be pitied. Plus, he didn't know the circumstance of incredible coincidence and stereotype; one that occurs all day every day, but just enough out of sight so guys like me can still function with hope.

Later, upon reflection of the day, I was thankful he trusted me enough to choke down his pride, and I marveled at the complexity, and relativity, of emotional pain and economic circumstance.

For Aaron's sake, I had to ask for repayment.

"Pay me back whenever." I said as I pretended to dig in the cabinet.

"Yeah... thanks," he replied, before disappearing into a kaleidoscope.

PART FOURTEEN

WHISPERED IN THE WINDS

Pop wrote two poems to me and Mary Beth for our wedding. I never really thanked him. I was a young knucklehead and viewed the cheesy, bi-fold frame with the encased poems as the meager offerings of a man with few material means – especially as it was presented in the company of Waterford crystal and Pottery Barn kitchen gadgets.

I scanned the words back on November 10, 1990, amid the traditional gathering of family and close friends – women around the gifts, men around the food and beer – but didn't really read the poems for another 24 years, several months after Pop had left us.

We dutifully displayed the corny gift – out of the way, in the basement. When I finally read the words in 2014, I cried like a baby who'd dropped his Binky and had a full diaper. Pop had captured my heart and the essence of my being. I looked up, as one does to catch a person leaving a room, to thank him, but his spirit was light years away.

The poem was inspired by my marriage proposal to Mary Beth. I chose to bend a knee at my favorite place on earth down on the Aleshire farm in St. Mary's township, Illinois near the crick where my brother, our cousins and I spent thousands of formative hours. To this day – and forever – it will be the sanctuary to my soul. It's as if my spirit was spun out of the universe and grew up in a gooseberry bush, a patch of clover – or a buckthorn – and worked its way out of that place and into the sentient status of humanity. My Pop knew that. I didn't know he knew.

"Whispered in The Winds"

It is a quiet place
A lea beside a creek nearby a grove
A glen so quiet one can hear the voices
Of guiding spirits whispered in the winds

The whispering winds which hear
The gentle beat of guiding spirits hands
As they applaud the journey
Which you have started on

A journey very personal, yet sharing
Gathering friends and family to join
A series of events leading to one moment
Which can never be forgotten

A short moment of simple words
Which speak so eloquently
To the friends and family
Gathered to celebrate the journey

A journey from a quiet place
A lea beside a creek nearby a grove
A glen so quiet the spirits hear your hearts
And hear your thanks for their applause

The farm, and the lea beside a creek, nearby a grove, are always with me, but have become almost mythical as once-familiar faces and places are reclaimed by the heavens and the earth.

I know my journey will lead me back there to join the many voices of guiding spirits; the tribes of Sac and Fox, the settlers and farmers, the deer, raccoon, the sparrows and the quail, the bullfrogs and snakes, the crickets, ticks, and tadpoles in the stream.

Together, we'll all whisper in the winds.

PART FIFTEEN

CANADA FOR A THOUSAND?

Alex Trebek gave a toast to me and Mary Beth on the first of our two honeymoons. We were flying First Class to Montreal courtesy of her employer, Northwest Airlines, and the esteemed Jeopardy host from Sudbury sat across the aisle in 2B. I ordered champagne from the flight attendant 'to toast my bride;' Alex overheard and asked the whole front cabin to join in wishing us newlyweds a long and prosperous life together.

Well, he *was* across the aisle, and did give us a polite nod and a smile.

First Class air travel was old hat to Mary Beth, but for me it was the groom's gift that balanced the bridal registry. I had travelled extensively prior to marriage but primarily in the 'way back' of a family station wagon, via Jefferson Lines, or with too many college buddies in a vehicle of questionable reliability.

After our engagement, there was a running joke among friends of how Mary Beth brought flight benefits and good looks to the union, while my dowry was a crazy family who didn't even have a lake cabin. In truth, we both brought travel industry connections to the relationship. As Mary Beth facilitated VIP trips to London, or Hong Kong in the "Far East," I was doing freelance travel brochure-writing in the

"Mid-West" for FirstLine Tours, a company that specialized in putting widows on motorcoaches bound for places like Medora, Ladysmith, and Silver Dollar City.

The FirstLine affiliation did pay off when Lois Weidner – the woman who got me the writing gig – arranged a suite for us at Le Versailles Hotel in Montreal. Most people don't think Canada from Minnesota for a Honeymoon – especially not in November. But most folks don't know that Montreal is due East, not north of St. Paul. It's not like we were headed to Flin Flon – plus, we had plans for Ireland six months later.

Thanks to Lois, the staff at Le Versailles had prepared a lovely gift basket along with elegant four-color, high-gloss brochures in the sitting room of our suite; it was one of those nice touches of panache for which the French are so famous.

My great grandparents, the LaBontes, hailed from Quebec, and 'Le Club de Hockey Canadien' (the Montreal Canadiens) were my favorite NHL team besides the North Stars. I actually knew why they were nick-named 'The Habs;' it's short for 'Les Habitants', the original settlers from districts west of Paris. One would think I'd have a rudimentary feel for the city, but I didn't. Almost everything was in French, except the numbers, and they were all wadded up in bundles of ten.

We'd been scrambling for a week with the groom's dinner, wedding, reception, and gift opening and barely caught our breath before heading to the airport. We were thankful that, back then, going to Canada was like going to Michigan, and we didn't have to round up passports and seven other forms of I.D.

When we got to the suite at Le Versailles and dropped our bags, it finally sank in that we were really married. Our eyes met, and we shared a brief moment of 'holy crap, this is forever,' then set the timer on the camera for an old-school selfie to capture the moment.

I picked up the visitor's pamphlet for some ideas of what to do on a Sunday in November in Montreal, Quebec. The stylish, multi-lingual guide mocked my hand-typed bus tour flyers on goldenrod copy paper; the condescension was infamously French.

I opened it anyway and started reading, "Let's see, there's the Orchestre symphonique … the Basilica de Notre Dame… Old Montreal…" then tried to nonchalantly add, "huh… the Canadiens are playing the Nordiques at the Forum tonight... or we could…"

"Oh, let's go to the hockey game!" Mary Beth chimed in.

I knew I'd married well.

My Minne-SOH-ta accent gave the cabbie an opportunist's grin as he started a meter in his head that would double the cost of the ride – maybe triple with the exchange rate.

"Où allons-nous… where are we going?" he translated.

Mary Beth spoke over me to crush his illusion of a triple-rate fare, "To the hockey game. We rode past the Forum this afternoon and saw there's a game tonight."

Pre-Uber cabbies hated short rides, and it was about 2 miles to the Forum, an arena that was to Canadians what Wrigley, Fenway, or old Yankee Stadium was to Americans. The Habs left it for the Molson, now Bell Centre in 1996 and despite twenty-four Stanley Cup Championships, haven't won another since.

I gazed at charming, European-like architecture as light snow fell, and I held my new wife's hand. The driver did his best to crush the mood as he mumbled the only French words that aren't romantic and did jackrabbit starts and stops to within a block of the rink where we sat in a logjam. He was too angry to wait and jerked the cab into the oncoming lanes as traffic waited for the turn signal, then hammered the gas pedal and nearly put us on two wheels as he turned, barely in front of the now-approaching vehicles. A loud thud pounded the back of the car – someone threw an ice chunk at us – then he gassed it again, fish-tailed the cab, and slid into an alley.

"Merci. Au Revoir…" he said urgently.

"Nice hustle!" I said as I fumbled for my wallet to pay him, "How much?" Mary Beth knew the thump came from hitting another vehicle and was tugging on my arm to get me out and let him speed away.

His anxious eyes were fixed on the rearview mirror, "Rien. Nothing. Aller! Aller! Go!"

Mary Beth was shaking her head and mine was in a daze as he spun the tires and threw gravel before I had a chance to tip him.

A block later my oblivion would end. I had been in the sports marketing business for a full nine weeks and was ready to do some wheelin' and dealin' with the local docket peddlers. The Habs' Provincial neighbor, the Quebec Nordiques, were in town with a former Canadien and fan-favorite, Guy Lafleur, so the ticket supply was tight. We approached a man waving two tickets in the air.

"J'en ai deux, j'en ai deux," Rusty, a classic looking scalper, repeated.

I launched into the vetting process, "Are they any good?"

"Are ze any good?" He smiled and repeated back. "You're American?" Rusty was the happiest 'Habitant' we'd met so far. "You been to ze Forum?"

"Nope. Our first visit." I kept working him.

"Ah, welcome! You'll love it. I have two left, beautiful seats. Section 3, Row K, you know, a, b, c, d..., at the Blue Line."

"Sounds great." The vetting process ended.

After a short welcome speech from Rusty, we paid sixty bucks American, thanked him, and headed into the most legendary hockey rink in the world.

It felt like every year since 1924 inside the Montreal Forum. The place reeked of history... and smoke. The Indoor Air Act hadn't emigrated, and a blue-gray haze hovered in the upper half of the building to give it the nostalgic look of a newsreel from a 1950s boxing match. We pitied the person who had to clean the dozens of championship banners that hung from the rafters – if that person existed.

The capacity was 3,000 more than our Met Center and even a bit bigger than the massive St. Paul Civic Center, and with four levels of seats towering into the cloud, it felt as big as both. An usher asked if we needed help, saw Section 3 Row K, then pointed in a foreign language to our seats. He pointed up, way up, to Section 403.

We were happy to be young as we scaled the stairwells then emerged to find ourselves amid a sea of Nordique Cyan Blue. A charter from some tavern in Quebec City had two no-shows, and sweet ol' Rusty paid the organizer $5 each for the leftovers he served to us at a tidy profit.

There were twelve rows in Section 403. K is the 11th letter in the alphabet. As the saying goes, "the seats weren't heaven, but you could see it from there." We could also see that there was no banner cleaner. Fortunately, Mary Beth is a "fun is where you take it" person and the Quebecers welcomed us as if we could speak their language.

One dialect we all shared was LaBatt Blue, a brew that had limited distribution in 'The States' but was within arm's reach of our seats – right behind Section 403, Row L.

Way down on the rink, Guy Lafleur's signature blond hair-flow waved like a flag for Quebec sovereignty as he took to the ice for warmups. The province roared in united cheers for the only Hall of Famer to come out of retirement to play again. The former Canadien and current Nordique was one of the last 7 players in the league to be grandfathered-in after helmets became mandatory in 1979, and a helmetless player added to the night's retro atmosphere.

The challenge of not knowing the language turned to fun as our charter pals and the scoreboard helped out with bilingual translations.

To beg a ref for a hooking call in the U.S., you put your hands out in front of you like you're grabbing a rope, then pull it toward you a couple times as you yell, "Hook! Hook! C'mon ref!" It's exactly the same in Quebec, except they shout, "Accrochet! Accrochet! Allez, ref!"

The French cheers and jeers sound the same as English when blended on a TV set but were a blast to experience live – especially in a back-and-forth game that Montreal won in overtime. Lafleur got a *mention d'aide* – an assist – one of 1,353 points in his career.

Game night was the highlight of the trip, but before our first honeymoon was over, we toured the Basilica de Notre Dame, some quaint shops, and cafes, and took the requisite hansom cab ride through Old Montreal.

Afterwards, Mary Beth apologized to the two-thousand-pound horse for the difficulty of pulling us around by handfeeding him carrots and petting his nose. It was appropriate

– perhaps inevitable – to have the first in hundreds of animal-loving stops in our marriage be on our first honeymoon.

My wife recognized in Montreal that – for the most part – she would be the savvy, and I the rube in our relationship. She does all critical negotiating for us – cars, houses, etc. – but I swear she makes a sport of watching me get Opie Taylored by scalpers. She lets me keep trying, like we're playing horseshoes, and the only time she stepped in was in Berkeley, California for 'The Big Game'... but that's another tale.

The last game played at the Montreal Forum was in 1996. The emotional good-bye was made even more so as event organizers trotted out a line from the gallant World War I poem *In Flanders Fields* by Canadian author, John McCrae. The poem inspired world-wide Poppie sales for Veterans – an effort led in Minneapolis by my French-Canadian grandmother.

On the final night at the Forum, they recited the line: "*To you from failing hands we throw the torch; be yours to hold it high,*" as all living captains of the Canadiens handed a ceremonial torch down the line till it reached the current captain, who carried it to the new arena the next day.

Thirty years after Alex Trebek gave us a polite nod to acknowledge our marriage, Mary Beth and I still have a fondness for our neighbors to the north. We maintain the old-fashioned gender roles we like – and ignore the ones we don't. She lets me be stubborn when it's harmless, I let her drive almost all the time, and we share the TV dinger. We pass chivalry back and forth like a torch – or a soft-touch drop pass from Guy Lafleur.

Part Sixteen

13 DAYS IN OCTOBER, PLUS ONE

Everyone knows about the Cuban Missile Crisis and how, for thirteen days in October of 1962, humanity was dancing on the threshold of self-annihilation. The Kennedy brothers, John and Robert F., played nuclear chicken in a test of wills with a Russian Socialist named Nakita Khrushchev.

Our civics classes taught us how Jack and Bobby saved the world – and Nikita's hide – by cutting a side deal that scrapped NATO's arsenal in Turkey and kept communist missiles out of the western hemisphere.

There was fallout from the nuclear exchange however, even without so much as the launch of a bottle rocket. We humans have lived in a perpetual end-of-the-world scenario ever since; one that probably contributed to Baby Boomers' pathological protection of their children, and to a society where emotional safeness has surpassed oxygen as a life requirement.

Twenty-nine years after the missile showdown, thirteen October days delivered another struggle for world supremacy, and hell froze over. My wife was diving at the Great Barrier Reef and missed it all. She missed the 1991 World Series; a battle of athletic wills featuring Atlanta vs. Minnesota in what many consider to be the most intense in baseball history.

It concluded with a 10-inning, 1-0 shut-out that felt even closer than the score. Jack Morris pitched all ten frames for the Twins and a guy couldn't help but let his heart out to Braves fans whose club had the bases loaded in the 8th inning.

After a hundred centuries of residents in the western hemisphere living and dying in competitive harmony with nature, it took just two centuries for people to threaten nature itself, and to act as if life and death is balanced by the evening's entertainment. I'm as guilty as anyone.

The series began on Saturday, the 19th with game one at Metrodome, Minneapolis. Pre and post-game festivities were conducted two blocks away at The Little Wagon restaurant. This was not only convenient to the stadium, I happened to have a monthly tab at "The Wagon," and was close friends with Hall of Fame bartender Mike 'Ollie' Oliver, and – more importantly – with the bouncer, the late, great Mike 'Porkie' Pikala who let me cut through lines that wrapped around the block like I was Frank Sinatra at Toots Shor's place in New York during the Yankee dynasty.

A co-worker and former VP with the Twins, Mark Weber, granted me four of the most valuable tickets in Minnesota sports history. With my top advisor halfway 'round the world, me and my cadre of buddies had no deterrent to our revelry. We arrived early and stayed late.

Twins wins in the first two games on Saturday and Sunday led to grueling post-game celebrations that were magnified by a 9:00 a.m. meeting on Monday. Fortunately, the work turned into more playtime as we rehashed the weekend victories as if relief pitcher Rick Aguilera had saved civilization from radioactive debris.

Atlanta retaliated to take the next three games in Georgia, which led to late-night lamenting and second-guessing of our administration's strategic maneuvers. By day seven of '91's thirteen, I'd slept about the same as Bobby Kennedy in '62.

On day nine, Kirby Puckett almost single-handedly won game six by slashing a triple in the first inning, stealing a home run in the third, then blasting a walk-off dinger in the 11th. I was so tired I would have traded places with Khrushchev.

There were two naps on the Sunday of game seven. The first at 5:00 a.m., the second at about 2:00 pm. They were separated by a gallon of water and a short walk from the bedroom to the living room where I laid on the floor with a pillow and fell asleep before I could reach up to turn on the remoteless television set. I did make it back to the restaurant for pre-game, and somehow mustered the energy for the post-game marathon.

Age, gender, race, political affiliation, faith, Chevy or Ford didn't matter that night as we hugged and high-fived and danced in blocks-long conga lines while the pubs stayed open far beyond legal closing times. The streets of Minneapolis were overflowing with the harmonious joy of being the most supreme game players in the world.

Mary Beth left town on October 18th. She phoned from Queensland, Australia as I was laying, exhausted, in the living room with my arms and legs spread like I was going to make a snow angel – or be drawn and quartered.

"Just got back from the Reef," she exclaimed. "It was gorgeous!" She then went on to tell me of kangaroos, koalas, and the personal time she got to spend with a celebrity wombat named Patrick Thomas.

It was only the second time we talked since she'd left. Our cellular devices at the time were as big as World War II field phones and a minute of mobile airtime cost about the same as a nuclear warhead. Even "land line" calls that flew across the water to international destinations cost ten bucks a minute when the average wage was ten bucks an hour (it's about $28 today), so we had a short chat.

"Well, we'll be back on Tuesday. I'm dreading the flight from Sydney to L.A. Looks like we'll be up front, though," she said.

The thought of 13 hours in a First-Class airline seat while someone delivered endless food and booze sounded like heaven to me.

"What's going on there?" She continued. "Did you pass out much candy last night?"

"I passed out, alright, but not much candy," I replied. "It rained yesterday, froze, then started snowing. I've been shoveling all day. We have more than two feet and it's still coming. The streets are littered with buried vehicles. Plus, Mike Weidner lost part of his fingers in a snowblower last night, so I went over to help him out." I paused to catch my breath, then said. "Oh, the Twins won the World Series the other day."

I was laying on my back in the living room for the second time that week. Her call came on the 14th day, November 1st. The thirteen days of October, 1991 concluded with a paralyzing Halloween blizzard just five days after the historic game seven.

The streets that had hosted the revelers and a ticker-tape parade three days earlier lay beneath a thick blanket of snow, with an inch of ice as the bedsheet. Nature would not be threatened. The previous season was history, in a hurry.

Another 29 years later – 58 after humanity gave itself a stay of self-execution – the nice, Minnesota harmony would turn to angry protests, then ravenous riots, gratuitous looting, the torching of a Police precinct, and damage to 1,700 businesses after a bad man callously killed another who he was supposed to detain.

The four days of mayhem felt more like 13 as Mayors babbled senselessly, our Governor acted tough, his National Guard sat in the on-deck circle, and we all watched the once supreme city burn.

Thirteen days in any October – in the years 1962, 1991, or 2020 – are all tiny specs on a timeline. The Game Sevens, the gratuitous looting, even the threats of global obliteration become microscopic footnotes to the games people play.

The Braves of Atlanta borrowed their name from indigenous peoples who roamed the would-be streets of Minneapolis for more than ten thousand years with a 'conscious rationality' that had no fear of nuclear proliferation, no need for salted streets. The early tribes and the streets were preceded by 150,000 bedsheets of ice in an Age-of-Nature far more powerful than our contrived Ages of Industry and Technology.

The ice gave way to animals and hunters. Hand-crafted arrows became intercontinental ballistic missiles. The weapons and toys, the people and places, are temporary intrusions on Nature's landscape – in a Universe that shall not be played.

The games are fun while they last; the seasons keep changing forever.

PART SEVENTEEN

HALL OF FAMER

I owe Lute Olson.

The once-famous collegiate basketball coach was the centerpiece of a bet I made at Don & Charlie's Supper Club in Scottsdale. For five years in the 90s I spent the month of January in Arizona working the Phoenix Open – and Don's was my favorite kitchen. The bar was pretty nice, too. Prior to closing in 2019, the place had one of the most valuable private sports memorabilia collections in the world and attracted a cavalcade of celebrities during the golf tournament and for baseball spring training.

I'd visit at least twice per week; the posted business hours of 4-10:00 p.m. were perfect for a guy who started work at 7:00 a.m. and kept going til the last client had been thoroughly wined and dined.

One particular evening, my client du jour departed at nine o'clock, leaving me to catch a few stories from owner Don Carson's regular clientele that had dwindled to about a half dozen. The usual suspects were mostly expatriates to The Valley of the Sun. They were restauranteurs, financial advisors, attorneys, and realtors who were allowed to hang out past the self-imposed 'Last Call' at nine-thirty, and for as long as the staff was still cleaning and prepping for the next day. The nine-to-eleven patrons had the best conversations - and the place was free of tourists and vacationing friends from back home in some Midwestern state, east coast borough, or Canadian province.

It wasn't always sports, but on this night their banter turned to basketball and analysis of whether Lute Olson's Arizona Wildcats could build on their visit to the Sweet Sixteen in the previous year's NCAA tournament. The gathering of five men and two women went quiet when I grabbed a pause in their debate.

"I have a bet for you all," I offered in a "I know something you don't know" tone.

At 33 years old, I was at least a decade younger than the regulars of the upscale, throwback supper club that served red meat and post-war nostalgia with Sinatra and Tony Bennett. The regulars knew my face as new, and as the youngster working at the golf tourney who usually didn't speak until spoken to.

"Alright. Whatta ya got, kid?"

As time went on, I got called 'kid' a lot, and liked it.

"I'll bet a round for the bar against my tab that nobody here can tell me where Lute Olson played college basketball."

There's no way my per-diem could cover a meal and seven drinks at a fashionable Scottsdale establishment, so the bet was a Lee Trevino move. 'Super Mex' was one of the best and most popular pro golfers of his era, and a quote machine. As a young man, he was known to hustle country club members in Dallas.

"Putting for fifty grand on the tour is nothing," Trevino would say. "Pressure... is when you're putting for ten bucks with only five in your pocket."

Bar bets, remembrance challenges, and know-it-allness was way more fun in the days before everyone had the universe in their pocket - even though there was almost never a way to prove who was right, (that's why Guinness created the Book of Records, by the way). There was an integrity to the debates that were usually decided by de-facto juries who would judge the evidence and credibility of witnesses.

When the jury was hung, plaintiff counsel would offer a second closing argument, "I know I'm right. Go look it up!"

Followed by the defense, "No. You go look it up!"

Don's regulars silently pondered possible outcomes and the shared risk, then nodded, "OK. You're on."

The women shook their heads. Liz looked around and rolled her eyes, "...the things you guys remember..."

Patty chimed in, "...and will bet on," she exclaimed. "Whatever... count us in."

I was feeling pretty good when the first three guesses were for Iowa, then started to feel Trevino's pressure from a guy named Al, who said, "Everyone thinks he's from Iowa cuz that's where he made his name coaching..."

My eyes thinned. In bar bets, there's always that S.O.B. who knows stuff you shouldn't know. I figured my goose was on a rotisserie.

Al finished, "...but Lute played ball at Long Beach State,"

My cheek bones went high and filled with smug. "Nope." I smiled.

Al was doubtful. "What? No?"

"No, sir. That was his first college *job*."

Now I was in the clear. There was just one guy left, Phil, and he hadn't said a word. I assumed he didn't know anything about basketball and was counting on the others for a free drink. Then he started to speak with an authority that puts assumers in their place.

"Lute Olson is from North Dakota. He went to a little Lutheran college."

My heart sank.

"His name is short for Luther."

The smug in my cheeks turned to stroke. Holy crap, Phil knows even more meaningless stuff than Al.

My boss - who introduced me to the restaurant - was gonna laugh at me, and my wife was gonna kill me for wasting a hundred bucks.

Phil was very deliberate as he put the final basting on my goose. "Lute Olson... played at... a little-known school in the northland..."

"Enough, enough. Get on with it, Phil," I thought.

"Mayville, North Dakota," he finished.

Seven heads simultaneously turned to me. Surely such a confident and obscure response was no guess. He had me beat and Angel, the bartender, started taking orders.

"Lute did play in Mayville...." I sulked as cheers went up.

"BUT...." I broke their revelry, "only on the playgrounds."

Phil sensed the ace up my sleeve and grinned as Al protested. "What are you talking about?"

I continued. "He was raised in Mayville and won a high school state title there, but Robert Luther Olson was a three-sport star and male athlete of the year at little-known Augsburg College in Minneapolis... my alma mater."

They all groaned at the overwhelming evidence. The middle name thing closed the case and the gracious losers even ponied up for Angel's tip. I earned a free steak and got to brag rather than grovel to my boss and wife.

Moreover, it was an unofficial induction as a 'regular' and would lead to what would become as close as I get to a hall of fame. I came to be friends with the staff and owner Don Carson – whose family founded Carson's Ribs in Chicago - and my image was featured prominently on the wall of the bar amid autographed pictures of people like Arnold Palmer, Hank Aaron, John Elway, and Billie Jean King. It hung right below Joe DiMaggio.

When I'd return each year for work at the Phoenix Open, with family or friends, Don would greet me with tongue-in-cheek flattery: "People keep asking, who's the guy above Pic?"

My photo on the wall, however, had nothing to do with the Lute Olson bet. One of the nuances of Don & Charlie's was that there was no Charlie, but Don would constantly make up excuses for why his 'partner' wasn't at the restaurant on any particular night.

During those pre-child days when Mary Beth and I both travelled a lot, I would go from 45 consecutive days of work in Arizona, to four days in Curt Blanchard's ice fishing house on Lake of the Woods along the Canadian border. The sunworshippers were aghast that anyone would drive two miles from shore on frozen water and further amazed that I looked forward to a 100-degree reduction in temperature. Don, with more tongue-in-cheek, told me to "send a postcard."

The landscape out across Lake of the Woods resembles Antarctica and was a perfect backdrop for Don's postcard. It was minus fifteen on the lake, but I dropped my parka hood, donned a D&C's hat, and held up a fresh-caught walleye* so one of the boys could take my picture. After a trip to Pro-Ex Photo Shop (as in a retail outlet that developed film from actual cameras) I had the photo enlarged and signed it for Mr. Carson:

*"Charlie's fish, but he's back behind the fish house sitting
on a toilet seat over a pickle bucket.
Best to all."*

Don put it on the wall next to the bar and the DiMaggio
references started the next time I returned.

The photo was a fun conversation piece for whenever I'd
bring new clients, family, or friends to Don & Charlie's. I was
hosting a newly-promoted region manager named Cindy one
Friday when PGA golfer, Fuzzy Zoeller, came in with a dozen
or so friends from around his home territory of Floyd's Knobs,
Indiana. They were celebrating two good days of golf that had
him near the top of the leaderboard.

M&M/Mars, a Phoenix Open sponsor, and our client at
the time, is a progressive company and Cindy was a glass-
ceiling-breaking, rising star back before women dominated
marketing departments and new hire rosters. She played her
cards professionally close to the vest and would typically leave
a dinner meeting right after the meal.

Cindy had a child with a female partner at a time when
Korean War veterans still dominated corporate boardrooms.
Don had heard conversations from her co-workers.

When she excused herself to the restroom, he asked me,
"What do you think of Cindy?"

I paused for a long moment. "Uhh... you mean her non-
traditional family?" I asked.

We looked each other in the eyes and shared another
awkward moment. "No... I guess not," he said. "You like
working with her?"

"She's the best," I replied.

He set the two of us up in the four-person "power booth" in the lounge.

The welcoming atmosphere had Cindy at ease at an hour usually reserved for regulars and late-arriving celebrities. We were enjoying tactical conversations about how to sell even more candy and ice cream when she pointed toward Zoeller's group. "It's after 10," she said. "Shouldn't he be getting some sleep?"

"Probably," I said, then asked Angel for a pen and paper.

On the paper I wrote, *"You won't be worth a shit tomorrow anyway, so here's another round - compliments of M&M/Mars. Give our tent on the 18th a wave as you go by."*

I showed it to Cindy. She laughed and said, "This is great. I'm buying."

The server took the note back behind the accordion wall that gave Fuzzy and friends some privacy. The room went quiet as he read the note aloud to his friends, who laughed and cheered.

The next day, Zoeller hit to the opposite side of the 18th, but walked across the fairway to genuflect at the crowd of candy buyers in our corporate tent who roared in approval as Cindy smiled about "incremental impressions."

I shook the basketball coach's hand once in a reception line at an Augsburg College fundraiser. He wouldn't have known me from Adam; but Robert Luther Olson set a pick for me that opened a lane to countless memories at a home away from home, and I owe him.

My 'Hall of Fame' is all closed up. May he rest in peace, in his.

PART EIGHTEEN

IT AIN'T OVER, TIL IT'S OVER

The Palmer House Hilton hotel in Chicago is a temple to the intricate opulence of the Gilded Age. Corinthian columns rise from floors of Persian carpet, past marbled tables and paintings by Monet, up to intricate cornices that buttress ceilings festooned with Tiffany chandeliers and elaborate frescoes by Rigal. It all culminates as an abridged version of the Sistine chapel.

In 2021, the fancy joint was 300 million bucks in the hole.

The precious rugs, big pillars, and swanky roof has insulated overly privileged drinkers of martinis, Manhattans and old fashioned gimlets for 150 years. The luxurious hotel, and others like it, seem opposite to the concrete floors, picnic tables, and exposed airducts of the warehouse brew pubs preferred by contemporary imbibers. Tom Collins and his colleagues seem to have given way to modern-day Sam Adams and a slew of crafty new names for booze.

The GenXYZ folks are clever, that's for sure. Our modern wit also reveals state-of-the-art petulance that mocks life in the Gilded Age with parodies of everything from monogamy to civil disobedience, and faith to freedom. Philology meets fill-ology with names like 'Polygamy Porter', 'Arrogant Bastard', 'Yeastus Christ', 'He'brew', 'Gandhi-Bot', and 'Brew Free or Die'.

My first trip to the Palmer House came as a vote of confidence from a boss who had the assurance of a mother bird. He tossed me from the nest to fly to Chicago by myself and deliver a major marketing pitch to a vice president and 12 regional directors of Mars, Inc., an international food manufacturer.

The group managed hundreds of millions of dollars in product sales and millions in promotional budgets. It was a crucial opportunity to land a nationwide program.

A pressed suit, discriminating tie, new belt, and shiny shoes couldn't cloak my gaping mouth at the historic property as I – pretending to belong – strolled past the velvet seats and up the Cinderella staircase. Some years later, my nephew re-captured the emotion I was feeling when he sent a family picture from inside a noted Parisian jeweler with the inscription, *The Clampetts come to Cartier!*

The Grand Ballroom at the Palmer House is just that, and has hosted luminaries like Mark Twain, Charles Dickens, Oscar Wilde, and every president since U.S. Grant. Current stars and past greats of entertainment such as Ella Fitzgerald, Judy Garland, Louis Armstrong, and Liberace have graced its stage.

I promenaded past the great hall to go stake my place in a corporate meeting room. There were no computerized projections of PowerPoints in those days, so Palmer's meticulous staff had perfectly positioned an overhead projector next to a podium. The refreshments, including strategic placement of client brands, were laid out on white linen, and organized for easy access by attendees. I was ready to go and thanked the team for setting the stage.

In my stylish leather briefcase that Mary Beth had secured on a trip to the "Orient," were 24 transparencies – two per region. Each skillfully separated by a sheet of goldenrod copy paper that was numbered and annotated with a transitional comment to let me glide like a hawk and pick off the prey one quarry at a time with peck after peck of precision research. I carefully extracted the presentation from the case and removed the protective folder. Attendees arrived early, so I set down the contents to greet them as they entered.

We chatted and refreshed til the time was at hand. I stood before the lord of budgets and his 12 apostles of marketing to be judged.

Brief intro and overview... so far, so good... On to review the stack of plastic transparencies on the projector that would seal the deal.

I looked down at the sheets to see the load had shifted. Why hadn't I moved them to the podium before the guests arrived, I thought. No matter. Before gathering and straightening the sheets with a two-handed tap on the podium, I casually reached down to flip the switch, to shine the light, that would project my brilliance to all.

Plastic is slippery.

Less than a second later, it felt like the Last Supper for me as the apostles looked on. The mass of research slid from the screen, bounced off the edge of the cart, slapped the floor in multiple plops, and spread out like the Sudoku puzzle from hell.

My forehead lit up like a warning light atop the Hancock tower, my earlobes looked like cherry tomatoes, and the apostles did their gracious best to keep from howling in laughter at my brilliance. I awkwardly stepped around the podium, bent over, and desperately pawed at the jumbled numbers as I attempted to reestablish confidence and competency with a series of 'umms' and 'uhhs'.

The VP spoke up before every lower lip in the room was bitten clean through.

"Hey," he said. "Leave that shit on the floor and wing it. We'll look at the numbers later."

I stood straight just before every drop of blood had reached my head, then picked up a glass of water that shook in my hand like a Yahtzee dice cup. I took a pull, a deep breath, and looked around the room at faces that were smiling with me, not at me. The situation became irresistibly comical, and I had nowhere to go but up. It became another of life's blessings in disguise. I was forced to conversationally deliver information I knew quite well, rather than recite boring statistics from spreadsheets.

The VP approached me afterwards. "Ya done good... after the fuckup," he said with a grin. "I'll be talkin' to your boss."

We all belong at the Palmer House – if we want to be there. If we want to respect and appreciate the artisans' gilding rather than disrupt the beauty, if we want to admire the craft rather than spite the long-dead faces of those who commissioned the creation.

The Gilded House and the Crafty Brew Pub represent eras and worldviews of stark contrast, and yet, they're connected like parasitic twins of single mind. Both eras have viewed previous generations with egocentric condescension. We've always been like Caesar, who called those classic Greek pillars 'Romanesque,' or like Ugga the Homosapien, who called Mugga - the discoverer of flint and fire - a Neanderthal.

I'd amend any of a thousand screwups, bad decisions, and wrongful acts in my life. I would not, however, part with any of the life lessons. They taught me I'm not a victim unless I choose to be, and that envy is self-anger that destroys from within.

We'd all prefer a bit of compassion and a "Hoppy Ending" over a bitter conclusion.

PART NINETEEN

IT'S MY BIRTHDAY!

June 17, 1994, was one of the busiest news days in American history. I could have been anywhere in the world that weekend and wound up right where I belonged.

Seamus McCaffrey was a walking stereotype of a throwback Irish American in the '90s; from the brogue to a personality that could charm – or fight – at the drop of a tweed cap. We met in a hospitality tent at the Phoenix Open golf tournament in 1992. I was managing a sponsorship for M&M/Mars, and Seamus' clan of Celtic freeloaders had finessed their way into the corporate tent village. Their next objective was to con a tent manager – like me – into letting them stick around for free food and adult beverages.

Seamus wasn't shy with his charm as he approached to introduce himself. When he learned my name was Mike, his face lit up.

"Ahh, Michael. A good Irishman, no doubt," he said.

"About half." I replied.

He sensed half would be good enough for his con and smiled. "Seamus McCaffrey," he pretended to spit on his hand, then offered it to shake. The spit shake was once common, but little known today. It replaced the ritual of cutting one's hand with a knife to share bodily fluids in a solemn oath of bonding.

I shook his meaty hand and returned the glint in his eye to let him know managers of corporate hospitality venues are no strangers to roving opportunists. My silent hint of doubt was no deterrent to a man from Northern Ireland where "The Troubles" between Catholics and Protestants had been raging for hundreds of years.

To Seamus, quid pro quo was a way of life, and he shamelessly declared that I was now a friend to the owner of Seamus McCaffrey's Irish Pub in Phoenix, Arizona and that I, and my friends, would be treated accordingly. All he asked in return was a "wee rest" in our tent, and one pint for him and his friends who were visiting from the Auld Sod over in County Cork, (pronounced 'Cark').

I told them my mother-in-law's family was from Cork, near Blarney (I emphasized the word 'Blarney') and that I wasn't aware of a man from that region who could be quenched by a single pint.

"Aye..." they all smiled and nodded in hopeful agreement.

The subdued atmosphere of a tent full of competing grocery buyers needed a shot in the arm, so I instructed the clan that if anyone asked, they were guests of Seamus' foodservice distributor. He loved a good finagle and sent another grin with his eyes that said, "You and I will get along famously."

Two years later, he invited me to the Italy vs. Ireland World Cup soccer match in NYC, and for about a decade, our group of St. Patrick's Day revelers in Saint Paul would call down to his pub in Phoenix to kick the day off with a serenade of "Wild Irish Rose."

The World Cup match was to be played on my birthday, June 18, 1994, during a weekend that would become a harmonic convergence of historic sporting occurrences throughout the country. One of those events was the U.S. Open Golf Tournament at Oakmont Country Club near Pittsburgh, and a vendor had already invited me to join him for a go-anywhere Clubhouse Pass and once-in-a-lifetime opportunity to be up close as Arnold Palmer played his last competitive round in a major tournament.

Oakmont was Palmer's home course, and Arnie's Army faithfully followed him for two days, even as his last round had a feel of Thermopylae when he 3-putted each of the last five holes he played. The one-day score didn't matter; the adoring crowd gave him an extended standing ovation to applaud more than 40 years of entertainment, excitement, and selfless fundraising. The ever-gracious Mr. Palmer couldn't talk; his tears did the bidding of thank you, and farewell.

I wasn't there to see it.

New York City is perhaps the only place on earth that could host two professional league championships and the planet's most prominent competition – The FIFA World Cup – at the same time, without breaking stride.

The city never slept the weekend of June 17, 1994. It didn't have a chance. On Friday, Mark Messier was the de facto Grand Marshall of a ticker tape parade down Broadway after leading the New York Rangers to their first Stanley Cup championship in 40 years. Also, that weekend, Patrick Ewing and the New York Knicks were locked in one of the NBA's most epic championship battles with Hakeem Olajuwon and the Houston Rockets.

Meanwhile, the nearly identical flags of Italy and Ireland waved and streamed constantly through the streets. The pubs were packed with international visitors and local ethnics who gathered in pre-game cheer for their nation, or the 'old country' of their ancestors. On the flags, and in the pubs, a half-tone difference between Italian Red and Irish Orange was the only distinction.

Seamus was ecstatic as the Irish upset the favored Italians in a one-nil game that held the overflow Meadowlands crowd in torturous anxiety the entire afternoon. Tensions were later soothed with celebration and commiseration that spilled long into the night.

I wasn't there to see it.

On paper, Mary Beth and I had glamourous jobs for a young couple in our 30s. I was doing the Sports Marketing thing and attending high-profile events throughout the nation. Mary Beth was in sales with Northwest Airlines, and hosting VIP trips to exotic places like Thailand, Korea, Australia, Paris, London, and Amsterdam. She even hosted the Sister City contingent to Japan for the dedication of "Constellation Earth," St. Paul's monument gift to Nagasaki's Peace Park.

It all *sounds* glamourous, but our trips were usually marked by 12-hour workdays as we entertained clients, managed logistics, and schlepped around boxes of gifts and supplies. We rarely got to travel together. On the weekend of June 17, 1994, however, Mary Beth was taking a group to Anchorage, Alaska for an exclusive outdoor concert headlined by Don McLean… and I was invited.

As the concert's primary sponsor, Northwest employees and guests enjoyed back-stage access to meet the performers on a beautiful 70-degree day with North America's highest peak, Mt. McKinley (Denali today), and a full horizon of snow-capped mountains as a backdrop.

I wasn't there to see it.

Back home in Minnesota, I had worked my way through a dilemma that was an embarrassment of riches. In addition to the incredible invitations, I had an annual tradition and obligation to uphold. Each year my fishing buddy, Tony Nelson, and his family hosted The Wayne Nelson Memorial Fishing Tournament on northern Minnesota's *Dead Lake* to honor their father. "The Wayne" was held on Father's Day weekend, and Tony and I were the organizers.

Anticipation for the 3-day event would start to whip up on Thursday evening as teams checked in, halfway to the cabin, at "the roadblock": Jan's Bar in Freeport, Minnesota. The town was made semi-famous by Garrison Keillor as the inspiration for the fictional place, Lake Wobegon, on National Public Radio's Prairie Home Companion. Our inspiration, Jan's, was down the street from Keillor's preferred café.

We'd play golf on Friday then gather around a fire pit for a raucous Rules Interpretation Meeting. We often had guys fishing naked for good luck, Twins baseball on the radio, martinis at 'The Point' for Happy Hour, and dubious distinction awards throughout the weekend. In 1992 the Northern Lights lit up the sky as we returned from golf and we made our driver, nephew Jarrod, muscle my 4-speed stick Volkswagen van off into a field, so we could drag out the coolers and marvel at the infinite canvas of God's cosmic artistry.

As great as the other offers were, I couldn't part from the boys. The invitations to New York, Pennsylvania, and Alaska were gratefully declined. Then... in late May, Tony discovered cancer in his lymph nodes and the tournament was cancelled.

On June 17, 1994, there was no New York City pub full of Irish and Italians for me, no exclusive Country Club in

Pennsylvania with Arnie's Army, no Starry, Starry Night with my wife in Alaska, and no buffoonery with the boys in northern Minnesota.

But, hey, it was still my birthday weekend, and I most definitely had a reserved seat at my favorite watering hole, The Little Wagon Restaurant in Minneapolis.

"The Wagon" had an eclectic mix of patrons who were a bit more learned than your typical bar regulars. There were writers, editors, and press operators from the *Star Tribune* newspaper, financial executives, traders from the Minneapolis Grain Exchange, attorneys, cops, and occasional visits by elected officials from City Hall across the street. It wasn't uncommon for a game of Bridge to break out, or to engage a Pulitzer-winning columnist in discussion.

The 'Best Man' in our wedding, Mike 'Chief' Weidner, felt obligated to make sure I wasn't suffering "What If" syndrome, and joined me. He had put together a commemorative video that interviewed family, buddies, and our treasured coach and mentor, Jack Osberg.

The VCR tape was played at my bachelor party and concluded with one of my favorite movie clips from the Outlaw Josey Wales, wherein Josey (Clint Eastwood) eulogizes a friend with a matter of fact, yet ultimate compliment:

> *"This boy was brought up in a time of blood and dying, and never questioned a bit of it. He never turned his back on his folks or his kind... I rode with him... I got no complaints."*

One thing we knew on June 17, 1994: there were plenty of sports on the TV. In addition to the World Cup, Arnie's good-bye at Oakmont, and the NBA finals, Ken Griffey Jr. was chasing Babe Ruth's cherished single-season home run record – without performance enhancing drugs.

We didn't see any of them.

We couldn't. They weren't there to be seen.

Bob Costas cut away from what should have been his quintessential day of sports broadcasting to call the play-by-play of a White Ford Bronco on an L.A. freeway being followed by a dozen helicopters and half the State Troopers in California.

One of the nation's most successful sports & screen, cross-over celebrities, O.J. Simpson, was in the white truck, and exhibiting a curious reaction to his wife's and Ronald Goldman's tragic murders. The television coverage was on every channel and cast a bizarre spell of paralysis over us all that night as the entire nation watched the painstakingly uneventful episode unfold. Our obsession with celebrity had come of age, and the O.J. preoccupation overwhelmed every media outlet for many months to come.

A bar full of people who were more learned than most, just stared and mumbled at the television screens for hours.

Chief was tired of the bizarre and monotonous scenario and took a teasing shot at me, "Hey, happy birthday," he said. "How's that Alaska thing going for ya?"

"I would have picked New York, " I replied.

"Whatever," he concluded.

Seamus and I talked a month later. He regaled me with what I had missed in New York, and I told him he didn't know the half of it. His response was a mix of compassion and laughter.

"Ahh, Michael," he said. "The good Lord loves you. Hasn't He given you a brilliant story?"

A recurring line by Clint Eastwood playing Josey Wales came to mind. Depending on the inflection, it could mean anything from 'absolutely,' to 'what next?' I mused the line to myself:

"Reckon so…"

PART TWENTY

THE SPY WHO LOVED ME

I knew my wife, Mary Beth, was a wanna-be secret agent, but had no idea of the lengths to which she would go. She snatched personal property of the Clintons from the East Wing of the White House in July of 1994, and pinched it from right under the noses of staffers, then snuck it out past heavily armed secret service agents without dropping a bead of sweat.

We were there as representatives of the Mars family – as in m&m's and Snickers – to provide Dove Ice Cream bars to South Lawn guests of the First Family during a private Independence Day viewing of the Capitol fireworks. The opportunity came through an elite DC power broker named Thomas Boggs, who founded the law firm Patton-Boggs. He had close ties to the Democratic Party and also represented Mars, Inc., which is headquartered in nearby McLean, Virginia – right down the road from the CIA.

I was working for a promotional marketing firm who, like Boggs, did work for the Mars family. Our work included a national campaign for the world-famous confectioner and their recently acquired Dove ice cream brand.

In May of '94, Boggs got wind of our campaign and one of Tom's people called one of my people (I was in the restroom when a co-worker answered the phone), and before you could say 'Razorbacks', I was corresponding with a very gracious White House Deputy from Little Rock named Ann McCoy.

As manager of the campaign that operated 110 ice cream carts, it was my job to negotiate sponsorships and product placement, then coordinate equipment logistics to support distributors at major events like PGA golf tournaments, NASCAR races, the Kentucky Derby, and the Indy 500. The savvy lawyer saw an opportunity to scratch two backs with the same popsicle stick – my operations budget. His client, Mars, Inc., would get product placement at the White House, and his client, the Democratic Party, would get free ice cream for their yard party.

My boss and his client, a VP at Mars, thought it was a good idea, so I did, too. Our distributor in DC was also enthusiastic when I called to announce the sweet deal I'd lined up.

"Are you nuts?" he said. "I'm not gonna make one of my drivers fight 4th of July traffic in a reefer truck that has to get White House security clearance, all so a bunch of political cling-ons can get free ice cream. I'll sell you the product, but you're on your own after that."

Two months later, I was driving a 24-foot Penske box truck loaded with six ice cream carts and a bunch of treats for political cling-ons through bumper-to-bumper, DC traffic. Mary Beth was at my side playing the role of Siri and guiding us from Bethesda, Maryland to 1600 Pennsylvania Avenue with a half-folded map of metro DC in her lap.

I knew she'd read every Flynn, Clancy, le Carre', Sanford, and Ludlum book ever written, but I had no idea the sniffing dogs and Secret Service agents dressed in SWAT gear would incite the inner Mata Hari in my wife. As the agents began to inspect our rig, she went Greta Garbo on them with provocative questioning.

They attempted to maintain professional protocol, but her beauty, charm, and fiendish fascination for espionage was too much, and pretty soon the boys were chatting it up like tour guides. I don't recall which state secrets were revealed, only that the Clintons were identified as the most social family to ever occupy the place, and that the constant civilian traffic kept them on their toes.

"Yeah right," I thought, "my wife is scratching your dogs' ears like a household pet."

We passed the inspection, Mary Beth slipped them a box of frozen kickbacks, and we set off to meet Ms. McCoy and her handful of volunteers.

Ann McCoy was not only gracious, she was the Diva of Details. Her manner was so kind and thoughtful that, in the nation's capital, it could easily have been mistaken for quid pro quo influence, if not for the fact that she had nothing to gain but more details to manage.

We did the event again in '95. Ann was unaware of the previous year's caper, and during our initial planning discussion, asked me to tell Mary Beth she looked forward to seeing her again. I was surprised she remembered my name, let alone my wife's, but that was nothing compared to Ann's remembrance later that year.

I informed her that Mary Beth was seven months along in a high-risk pregnancy, and my nephew Jarrod Johnson, would be my able assistant. She offered heart-felt best wishes, and other than her asking how mother and baby were doing when Jarrod and I arrived on the 4th, that brief reference was the only time we discussed the pregnancy.

In October of '95, the first letter ever received by our young baby, Mary Murphy, came from the president of the United States. The compassionate note that welcomed her into this world was signed by Bill Clinton and was obviously the considerate work of Ann McCoy.

Jarrod and I had a great trip in '95 with visits to Old Ebbitts Grill, the Manassas battlefield, and a field trip to Georgetown where we had a photo-op on the front porch of the townhouse where Mom and Pop first met in 1951.

Jarrod was better at hauling ice cream than Mary Beth; he didn't woo any secret service agents, and he didn't steal anything from the White House… which brings us back to 1994.

Mary Beth and I went out a couple days early to see some sights; the Air & Space Museum, the Smithsonian Institution – she had to have a picture in front of the FBI Building – and we learned how to watch soccer at an Irish Pub referred by Seamus McCaffrey of Scottsdale – who had invited me to the Italy vs. Ireland World Cup match in New York City two weeks earlier.

After getting the carts and volunteers in place, we were able to take in the spectacle. The South Lawn is the green space that slopes at a gentle grade down from the White House, toward the Ellipse, the National Mall, and the Washington Monument. During World War I, sheep grazed on the South Lawn for Woodrow Wilson, to reduce lawn-mowing staff and to raise wool for the troops.

The President's back yard has a pretty decent view for the annual Capitol Fireworks on Independence Day, especially from the upper level of the portico, where Bill and Hillary stepped out for a brief welcome to the crowd. He was at a high point in popularity and the extraordinary charisma that got him elected was readily evident and captivated the guests.

As dusk turned to darkness, ramparts lit the sky and a soundtrack culminating in patriotic Sousa filled the air with a monumental postcard that would be seen on television by millions and in three dimensions by those of us grazing on the lawn.

By ten-thirty the show was over, and Ann McCoy was thinking of us as if she had nothing else to do. She anticipated the drudgery of Mary Beth and I driving the 24-foot Penske into vehicular gridlock and assigned a couple of staffers to take us on a behind-the-scenes tour of the White House, then let us relax in their office area until traffic had thinned.

Our hosts shared accounts of boredom and excitement in the East Wing – the hang-out for grunt staffers who perform the mundane duties of everyday life for America's First Family. As fate would have it – or in an act of cunning – Mary Beth sat in a chair next to a food and water dish for the Clinton's pet cat.

"Is this for Socks?" she asked with hopeful excitement that painted her as a giddy Midwestern housewife.

"It sure is," one staffer replied. "That's one of our jobs."

He went on to tell a few cat tales then turned to a cabinet to pull out a souvenir gift left over from Easter: an egg "signed" by Socks' paw print.

Mary Beth saw her opening. She surveyed the room in a split-second to take careful note of the eyes and levels of alertness of each staffer, then stealthily stuffed her pocket with a possession that was essential to a Clinton – a handful of Socks' supper.

On the way out, the White House staff was too tired and polite to screen us, and the secret service had already been seduced into unconditional trust. She walked out of the joint like she owned it.

Back home in St. Paul, Mary Beth laid out the smuggled stash for her King Pin cat, Bannister, who looked at the dish then dismissed the nuggets as a racketeer fence would reject fake diamonds. He was unimpressed by the pallet of the most powerful cat in the world and strolled away with that level of disinterest that makes you wonder whether cats are smarter than we are.

Mary Beth glared at the cat, then smirked. She had risked twenty-to-life at Leavenworth. She timed the heist and executed the sleight of hand in the East Wing to perfection, and she was cool as an ice cream bar with milk chocolate and almonds as she slipped out of the most heavily guarded place on earth with the contraband.

Ann McCoy and the Clinton staff could not have been more gracious and hospitable, and we were very thankful, but the votes in our home during the previous election had gone to George H. W. Bush and Ross Perot.

As she disposed of the evidence, Mary Beth grinned at the cat, "Good conservative kitty," she said.

PART TWENTY-ONE

FAMILY FEUD

I hate Cal Ripken, Jr. and his Baltimore Orioles.

Well, I tried to. We're about the same age and had a secret feud going on for 30 years. His dad tried to end it in Detroit one time, with an olive branch, but you know how feuds go.

The bad blood started when we were little kids. My favorite team, the Twins, lost to the Dodgers in the '65 World Series. Cal Junior's favorite team, the Orioles, beat Los Angeles in '66. A few years later it got more personal when his O's stole the 1969 and '70 American League championships from my Twins with crooked umps and some snot-nosed pitchers named Palmer, Cuellar, and McNally.

Then, in 1982, after Cal Junior had grown into a handsome, steely-blue-eyed glory boy with an MLB pedigree in an east coast market, he snatched the rookie of the year award from the hands of Kent Hrbek. Kent was born just down the road from me; we grew up together in the shadows of Bloomington, Minnesota's Metropolitan Stadium.

Hrbek's Kennedy Eagles baseball team faced our Rosemount High School squad in 1978. Everyone from our era and area acts like they know Hrbek. I was close to Kent – about 15 feet away – with my fingers hooked in chain-link, watching him bat against our Ace, who was a Division One pitching prospect.

When folks get to name-dropping, I tell them about the matchup.

"Our guy, Ralph, faced Herbie twice," I say. "Struck him out."

"Both times?" they always ask.

"No, just once."

"What happened the second time?"

"We're not sure, the ball hasn't landed yet."

The hardest part of feuding with Ripken and the Orioles was that they were historically known as good guys who espoused "The Oriole Way," a commitment to fundamentals that drew players and fans who were like-minded. To use a hipster word, Baltimore had "authenticity."

If I had known of Mike Rowe during the feud (he's the guy from *Dirty Jobs* and *The Way I Heard it*), I would have tried to hate him, too. He grew up in Baltimore near Cal and they're both close to the same age as Kent Hrbek and me. We all shared childhoods learning from parents, grandparents, and coaches about the authenticity of hard work, fundamentals, personal responsibility, and commitment to others; and we all became famous – except me.

As kids, when none of us were famous, the 'fundamentals' thing must have been getting to me because, for a while, I thought I might be inner-harboring a sub-conscious soft spot for the city of Baltimore, their people, and their ball club.

Then, Major League Baseball started building new, more modern and profitable places for big leaguers to play. They started in Bloomington by tearing down our beloved "Met" and moving the Twins to a Teflon bubble of a football stadium in downtown Minneapolis called 'Metrodome.' Guys like me and Herbie could sense what was coming next; Cal Junior and Mike Rowe got a palace called Oriole Park at Camden Yards.

People say Camden Yards is "the first retro ballpark." It's not retro. It's authentic, too. It's tucked into a cranny of Baltimore not far from the famed harbor – a cannon shot from where Francis Scott Key wrote the National Anthem. The exterior was crafted to fit in with its old warehouse neighbors and the interior was shaped with equally unique character. The ballyard sits precisely on the childhood stomping grounds of Babe Ruth, for goodness' sake. Every baseball park built since is a knock-off.

What's not to love about Baltimore, Camden Yards, those pitchers, Earl Weaver, Frank Robinson, Boog Powell, Brooks Robinson, Eddie Murray, Cal Ripken, and "The Oriole Way"?

A tainted childhood, that's what.

The idyllic summer pastimes of Cal Ripken Jr., Mike Rowe, and the kids of Baltimore, Maryland in the 1960s and '70s, often came at the expense of me, Kent Hrbek, and our Bloomington buddies. I carried the emotional scars for decades.

***

I met Cal Sr., kind of, at the now-defunct Ritz-Carlton in Dearborn, Michigan not far from the headquarters of Ford Motor Company. Ford sponsored the nearby Senior PGA Championship golf tournament where I was working, and I had to stay at the Ritz because it was the host hotel of the event, and in spite of the fact that Cal Ripken and those Orioles – who were in town to play the Tigers – were staying there, too. Cal Senior was coaching third base, and his other son, Billy, was playing 2nd base for Baltimore next to his older brother who played shortstop.

I spent eight Ritzy nights working with hotel staff to plan and administer customer hospitality events and was on a first-name basis with Penny in the lounge where our gatherings were held. One afternoon, I told her I was looking for something to do that night other than watch ESPN and asked if there was a shuttle to the baseball game so I could experience Tiger Stadium and – subconsciously – see all those Ripkens in one place.

There was just me, Penny, and a sunbaked guy who looked more like a farmer than a Ford Motor Company executive in the lounge. He seemed to be almost hiding as he stood leaning on a pillar at the far end of the bar near the little cubicle that housed bus trays, folded napkins, and silverware. The man heard our conversation and waved Penny down. They shared a few inaudible words before she returned.

"Mr. Ripken would like you to be his guest at the game tonight. You can pick up your ticket at Will Call."

My head shot down toward him, then back to Penny, where it settled with a quizzical look.

"That's Cal Senior," she whispered.

The feud had been dormant for a while and I figured he was gonna come down to sweet talk me into burying the hatchet once and for all, but he just leaned out from the pillar, gave me a quick "there you go" head-bob, then went back to sipping a small tap beer. 'Silent' Cal Coolidge had nothing on Ripken Senior.

I ended up on ESPN's SportsCenter that night. The seat from Mr. Ripken was right above the dugout but I got up after a couple of innings to explore the house of Hank Greenberg,

Charlie Gehringer, Alan Trammel, Lou Whitaker, Mark Fidrych, Mickey Lolich, Al Kaline, and a guy named Cobb.

The Orioles were in the hunt that year, but the legendary Tigers were not, so the outfield seats were empty. I walked to the top deck of center field and stood watching with nobody but a hot dog and a beer when Chris Hoiles launched a bomb to upper left center. Later that night, during TV highlights, it wasn't hard to pick myself out from the three of us. Earlier in the evening, it wasn't hard to walk over and pick up a souvenir homerun ball from the Baltimore Orioles – courtesy of Mr. Hoiles, and Cal Ripken Sr.

One would think an unsolicited peace offering, TV cameo, and homerun souvenir would be enough to end the feud, but I hadn't reached closure on the wounds of youth.

The Ripken feud did quiet down for a few years after the treaty of Detroit, however. Cal Junior didn't bug me, and I didn't bug him. There was a later flare-up though, when I happened to share a patio with another Oriole great, Mike Boddicker, who's a coincidental next-door-neighbor to a childhood, brother-like buddy. I tried to hate Boddicker, too. His enduring small-town-boy charm was just one more gentle twist-of-a-knife from the nest of the hard-to-hate Oriole flock.

But life marched on in our family after Cal Sr's. olive branch, and a few years later, in September of 1995, we were expecting a baby. Mary Beth had complications that put her on bed rest for three months. Day after long, hot, day was followed by another, each filled with incessant coverage of the first O.J. Simpson trial.

The media side-show set all tragedy aside as it made celebrities of the prosecution, defense, witnesses, and even the judge. The west coast circus was as far from the authenticity of

"The Oriole Way" as one could get. Newspapers were still the nation's journals in '95, and every rag in the country led with an 'OJ headline' for 473 days of the 474-day trial.

But Mary Beth was having a baby, and we managed to escape the onslaught of so-called news for a few days to welcome our daughter, Mary Murphy, at 8:07 p.m. on September 7th.

Mary Beth's mom, Jane Ann, had come to town to help ease us through the transition to a whole new life. She cooked meals, tidied up, and dutifully stacked the mail and newspapers during the three days we languished at the hospital after complications at birth.

As I sorted through the pile of bills, Direct Mail advertising, and O.J. Simpson headlines, I came across the first congratulatory gift after the birth of our daughter; it was another olive branch from the Ripken family – this time from Cal Junior himself.

I was thankful grandma had saved the newspapers – so we could honor the tradition of saving documentation from the date of a child's birth – but I shuddered at what empty sensationalism would welcome our daughter to this world. What petty, self-serving disagreement would the tabloids cling to on this day that was so special to me?

In big, bold letters that pushed courtroom antics to an inside fold, the headline on the day of our daughter's birth read: "2,131 – Ripken Makes Baseball History!"

Cal Ripken Jr. had played shortstop in every single Baltimore Orioles game from May 30, 1982, to September 6, 1995 – 2,131 games in all, and one more than the original 'Iron Man,' Lou Gehrig. He did what thousands before him could not do... he bumped sensationalism from the front page in an unprecedented act of perseverance.

The streak might have ended on July 26, 1993, with the birth of his son, Ryan, but the Orioles conveniently had the day off. Cal Jr. also played with a broken nose and several other maladies during a well-earned Hall of Fame career. During the streak, the Yankees played Derek Jeter and 18 other shortstops against the Orioles.

I was touched and humbled at the lengths to which Cal Ripken Jr. went to break the 30-year feud. My lone contribution was to let go of a tainted childhood by giving a souvenir homerun ball to a kid in Detroit wearing an Orioles jersey.

In 2001, when Cal homered in the last of his 19 All-Star games, I got a bit choked up for my old pal.

I love Cal Ripken.

PART TWENTY-TWO

WINNING

Winning isn't everything... or is it?
In the United States of America and our sibling Canada, sports dynasties are like sandwich shops; they're everywhere. The sheer volume is ironic; they blend the rare and exceptional to become commonplace.

One of America's little-known sports dynasties was a broomball team co-sponsored by The Little Wagon Restaurant and Buzz's Barber Shop in Minneapolis. For non-northerners, broomball is a game of Canadian origin invented by people who couldn't skate or handle a puck, so they dipped brooms in rubber to turn them into mallets, then threw a miniature soccer ball out on a rink to create a flat-footed version of hockey.

Our team had its intramural origins at Augsburg College, then evolved to state-wide competitive status as the Pilot's Club Bar. There were hundreds of teams at the time, and we were the 3rd best in the state one year then, the next, defeated legendary Fred's Tire of St. Paul for Minnesota supremacy.

One championship, however, does not a dynasty make. The Wagon's fabled status was achieved by winning the Minneapolis Senior Men's Outdoor Recreational League (South Division), every year from 1982 through '99. The Post

Office squad threatened our run a couple of times. The snow never interrupted their appointed rounds, but let's just say we redefined 'gloom of night' for them at a rink on one of the city's legendary lakes.

The greatest threat to our empire, however, came from the Rosen brothers of the Cedar Inn 3.2 beer and burger joint in our last year of competition. The Rosens recruited two lines of youthful ringers from the tavern and were within 10 minutes of dethroning us. The score was 2-1 when one of their little knot heads gooned me from behind. My teammate gooned the kid in retaliation, and after a miniature melee of boy-men in four layers of clothing slip-sliding into hog-piles, the ref declared the game "no contest" by walking to the parking lot and driving away. It didn't make the sports page.

Our nation's structure of youth associations and high school conferences offer easy access to extracurricular opportunities. Between schools and community centers, 90% of America's youth live within 20 minutes of a chance to do something other than loiter, or gape at a cell phone. But the playground rinks are empty, the gymnasiums quiet, and great dynasties aren't quite what they used to be.

One of my broomball teammates, 'Special Tim' McGlinch, lived two doors down. We gathered regularly in his garage to watch Minnesota Gopher hockey – yet another former dynasty that once drew the ire of hockey fans from Boston to Fairbanks.

Garage hockey-watching on a January night in Minnesota is not for the faint of heart. Tim would draw a martini glass in the frost on the window in his garage that I could see from our porch. This was his game-on "Bat Signal."

We'd gather under scale-size banners for every Gopher National Championship and Runner-up, courtesy of Roger, the garage's unofficial historian. A typical winter night would see the nails that had poked through the side walls tipped with white frost. Bob would share tales of his appearance in the Minnesota State High School hockey tournament when he played for an east side dynasty: the Governors of St. Paul Johnson – where a guy named Herb Brooks happened to make a name for himself.

High school hockey talk would lead to intense debates about which program was the greatest of all time. Eveleth, International Falls, Bloomington Jefferson? What about Cretin? The Raiders had a dozen private state titles before the public schools let them into the tourney. Charlie would tell us all to 'get over ourselves' when discussions got heated enough to melt the frost off the nails, then we'd agree that pound-for-pound, the Rams of tiny Roseau were the greatest, but overall, the nod had to go - grudgingly - to the Edina Hornets.

Tim had a framed picture of our broomball team that hung on the wall beneath the scale-sized Gopher hockey banners. I'd point to it, then remind the boys that, "Nobody – not even John Wooden's UCLA basketball Bruins – ever won 18 consecutive championships."

Historian Roger would heat up again. "If you're going to bring basketball into this," he'd say, "then we have to discuss the Grand Meadow girls who won 94 games in a row from 1929 to '39!"

Off-season garage sessions needed a theme, so we called ourselves a book club. Not the assigned reading, group discussion type – we'd just talk about things we learned from books: *Ax Throwing for Amateurs, Heisenberg's Uncertainty Principle, Sidewalks in Landscape Design.* Roger introduced: *Genghis Khan and the Making of the Modern World.*

Talk about a dynasty. The Khan set the standard for domination that progressed down through the ages and onto a frozen lake in South Minneapolis. Genghis had the biggest, meanest, and most broadminded empire ever. His Mongol hordes were ruthless, but they also gave soon-to-be-conquered rivals the opportunity to surrender, retain religious freedom, and become trading partners within the Silk Road network. We were never that gracious to the Rosen boys, or the mail men.

Our pond-based dynasty on behalf of a bar and a barber shop – a gin joint and a clip joint – was the apex of my athletic achievement. In high school and college, my buddies and I – like most of the nation's athletes who raised themselves on playgrounds back in the day – settled for 'signature wins' surrounded by demoralizing losses.

A signature win is a competitive game in which an underachieving team plays to its potential and defeats a team they weren't supposed to beat. This is not to be confused with the 'moral victory' where a sub-par team plays well and doesn't get crushed as badly as people thought they would.

Most of life is made up of the way we respond to the lessons of failure. We mix in the signature wins and moral victories from time to time, as we hope – just once – to play for a team of destiny.

Despite the rare-and-exceptional requirement, building a local sports powerhouse is no mystery. The ad could be posted in an online search: *"Wanted: passionate, mentoring coach willing to work long hours, weekends, and summers, for moderate pay. Must teach life and game fundamentals as the same, preach aggressiveness in competition, and humility elsewhere.."*

That's all it takes. Life and dynasties are simple. Work hard for a long time, respect others and whatever resources you have, avoid temptation, avarice, and envy. Simple.

When playtime is over, the folks from Eveleth, Roseau, and International Falls… Cretin, Jefferson, and Edina, will join the recreational man-boys of The Little Wagon & Buzz's Barber Shop broomball team.

We're all part of the same dynasty, one that always has been, and ever shall be.

PART TWENTY-THREE

TEN CENTS: A PITTANCE FOR HOPE

The slope from our friends' cabin in northern Minnesota down to the lake was steep, with a partially rotted, semi-winding wood staircase. Mary Beth and I were guests of the couple, and life was good. In addition to cabin invitations, we had interesting careers, a new house in a great neighborhood, and a young child who was both clever and adorable; yet we were feeling a bit adrift at the time.

We were navigating through the "seven-year-itch" stretch of our lifetime commitment. We were still young but approaching whatever "Middle Aged" is – when you want more out of life, and less, or maybe something different. When you want love to be automatic and everlasting but discover that it's fragile and very tough and requires hard work that must be performed again, and again after each mistake – but can't be taught.

Lessons can be learned, however, and itches soothed in a million ways: the taking of a hand while sitting in a pew; an extended embrace after the loss of a loved one, or the shared enjoyment of a child's silliness. Relief can come through a random act of kindness, the binding response to an attack on our nation that strikes too close to home and - perhaps most often - through the traditions, values, and collective experience of family that serve as safety nets to unconditional love.

We relied on them all – eventually - along with perpetual sacrifice and forgiveness.

It was nearing midnight, and everyone else at the cabin had retired for the evening. I stayed up with the owls and opted against navigating the staircase to sit by myself in an Adirondack atop the hill to reflect in the backwoods along with the moon and stars off the lake - then decided to challenge God.

God didn't back down.

I looked up at the heavens, closed my eyes, and asked - from the depth of my soul - for peace and balance. I asked for myself, my wife, and for every spirit I could comprehend at the time. It was one of those too-infrequent moments of complete self-confidence in one's intention.

I looked around at the beautiful pines, pin oaks, and conifers that filtered moonbeams down to a blanket of needles and cones, then spied a bird bath 20 feet away. It was partially blocked by one of the trees, and I interpreted it as a wishing well. It's easy to dismiss wishing wells as pools of superstition – or cynical revenue streams – but I see them more as reminders of the hope in our hearts that can be repurchased with a pittance.

With only ten cents in the pocket of my Bermuda shorts - and without hesitation or a break from the intentional mood - I flipped the dime off my thumb and as it was in mid-air, said, "There, send me a sign."

I wasn't asking God to deliver a specific message by placing the coin in the center of the would-be wishing well; I mean, it wasn't like the time I was sitting in the vice principal's office in junior high begging for immediate divine interruption of a phone call to my mother. I just flicked a coin, and hoped to be guided toward a more loving, purposeful life at some point in the journey.

Sometimes, God takes years... decades... to answer a prayer. Sometimes, a mysterious answer arrives in the time it takes a pittance to travel twenty feet.

The coin plunked dead-center in the birds' bathtub - a shot I couldn't duplicate with a thousand dimes.

I did that little snort thing through my nose - the one that pushes your shoulders back for a split-second and simultaneously makes you nod; then smiled and turned my eyes back up to a billion points of light.

I talked to God.

"Besides a really nice 'hello,'" I said aloud, "I'm not exactly sure what that means, but thank you."

PART TWENTY-FOUR

HEROIC

The most heroic moment of my life came at Gettysburg – Gettysburg Place that is – in a 55-plus housing development in Jefferson City, Missouri where all the streets are named for Civil War battles.

I'm no General George Pickett, and the circumstances didn't have the future of the Union, or the Confederacy hanging in the balance, but I did make a charge, there was precious life at stake, and my cause was unmistakably just.

I was picking weeds from the decorative landscaping around my in-laws' mailbox and cursing the clay and limestone grit Central Missourians call topsoil. As St. Louis is the Gateway to the West, Jeff City is the Gateway to the Ozarks. The city of 45,000 residents is an inviting blend of small-town charm and state capital activity, with a spectacular capitol building dominating its skyline the way The Gateway Arch does St. Louis.

The region's rugged topography begins at the capitol – along the Missouri River – and rolls an hour south to the largest man-made reservoir in the world, the Lake of the Ozarks. The picturesque scenery continues another 300 miles down through the Ozarkian entertainment mecca in Branson, past Walmart

World in Bentonville, and over the Boston Mountains to Fort Smith, Arkansas.

Our nephew, Aaron, was nine years old in 2001. Daughter Murphy was six and taking her first turn on a new "big girl" bike with mother and grandmother watching from lawn chairs in the driveway as the kids peddled out into the typically quiet avenue. Helmets were still optional gear at the turn of the millennium.

As a local, and being three years older, Aaron had established a riding course that was grandparent approved; down the driveway, left past one neighbor to the corner, then down into a parking lot across the street that served one of the city's many government administration buildings.

In Jeff City, and the Ozarks, hill meets hill, then transitions into hill. The entrance to the lot is no exception; it's a half-block long, fifteen-degree asphalt ramp that runs parallel to Gettysburg Place. The slope ends with a ninety-degree elbow turn into the lot itself.

Construction engineers got to use explosives to blast the clay and limestone until it was free of weeds and formed a deep box of ancient, exposed aggregate around the facility. Forty feet below the elbow was more of the same in another limestone box around another building.

Aaron had negotiated the hill and turn many times. It was Murphy's first attempt, but she had to keep up, and followed him down the ramp.

I had my plumber's posterior pointed toward the government as I worked on the weeds, dug around the mailbox, and wondered how Cole County, Missouri ever produced a single bushel of grain.

As I hunched, and muttered, and dug, our only child – then her mother and grandmother – sent up cries of anguish worthy of rebels in a Pennsylvania field. The "big girl" bike was new alright, with a feature she didn't know existed – hand brakes. Her cries intensified as the chain spun helplessly in reverse.

Weed picking duty was to be a brief deployment, so the laces of my well-seasoned Red Wing boots were dangling free of the grommets. I looked under my arm from the bent-over position to see a big girl bike gaining speed, and a little girl's terror keeping pace.

Football days as a defensive back came in to play as I executed a flawless step-and-turn that was far better than the one I used when Tim Gustafson of St. Thomas College scorched me for a TD on my first collegiate play from scrimmage (the touchdown was called back due to a holding penalty, but that's the only play I got that day).

Thanks to a shot of paternal adrenalin coursing through my veins, and thanks to my former coaches who were merciless in pursuit-angle drills, I could have run down Randy Moss on that day in Jeff City – even in untied Red Wing clodhoppers.

I picked an intercept point, then completed the forty-yard dash across the street and down the grade in Usain Bolt-like time to complete a one-armed scoop of Murphy from the two-wheeled demon just before it flipped and contorted like a riderless BMX entrant in an X-Games competition. The wheels kept spinning as it crashed into the trees that peeked above the lower lot.

The tiny sliver of time from decades ago still awakens butterflies that remind me I was within an eyelash of forever losing their kisses.

My actions at Gettysburg weren't really heroic, they were instinct meets training in a phenomenal coincidence. If I had been a lumbering lineman, a chess player, or an aficionado of the oboe, who knows what may have happened. With seven billion people in the world, anonymous, dramatic moments like these occur on a daily basis – not always with a quick-passing scare and comforting relief.

Our heroes come in many forms, including tragic.

Felicia Sanders bestowed heroic forgiveness on a deranged young man who murdered her son in a South Carolina church. I don't know how. I do know her mercy inspired many, while the deranged man's purpose was cast to hell.

James Allen Ward of New Zealand and the Royal Air Force climbed out on the wing of an in-flight bomber to extinguish an engine fire and save his crewmates. As the flyer was receiving the Victoria Cross award, Winston Churchill noted the man's discomfort.

"You must feel awkward and humble in my presence," Churchill said to Mr. Ward.

Ward nodded, and the Prime Minister added, "Then try to imagine how awkward and humble I feel in yours."

Two months later, Ward perished during another mission.

I struggled for decades with a personal dilemma regarding heroism during the Civil War combat at Gettysburg.

On the second day of that three-day struggle, supreme gallantry was displayed by the 1st Minnesota Regiment. The Confederates were about to overrun a position so strategically significant that the battle--and the tide of the entire war – hung in the balance.

Outnumbered five to one, Minnesota's Red Bulls, as they are still known today, counter-charged with no intention or expectation of return. They sustained a casualty rate of eighty-two percent, and historians agree "they are entitled to rank as saviors of their country."

The following day, 15,000 soldiers of the South, under the leadership of my great-great grandfather's nephew – General George E. Pickett – attacked across an open field in a desperate, ill-fated attempt to re-turn the tide. For more than half of them, it was the last mile.

As a Minnesotan named Pickett, I was conflicted for years by allegiance to state or surname, then later by the more relevant question of purpose. At some point, I arrived at a conclusion to honor the powerful courage of each individual, and to despise the weakness of hate that commands so costly a sacrifice.

Our spirits yearn for heroes – of love and in conflict – to shower with acclaim. We secretly hope to be heroes ourselves, as parents, friends, or citizens. These aspirations aren't necessarily born of selfish ego, but of a natural desire for relevance and purpose within life cycles that can trudge and toil their way into hopeless anxiety. And that anxiety can mutate into displaced distraction, rather than inspired pursuit.

But we know of the mother from South Carolina, and of another mother from Calcutta, Sister Theresa, whose worldwide influence began with the scrubbing of a foot.

Sprinting in untied Red Wings to save what was most precious to me was an instinctive responsibility – finding, or inspiring purpose and relevance amid the constant challenges of life is another thing altogether.

Our voices cry for the unity of many to justify the life of one. Our painful wails mutate into tragic, vicarious, political dysfunction.

Inspiration may be found in congregation, but relevance is the domain of the one. It becomes purpose when it is selflessly – sometimes heroically – given up to the many.

It is not, and cannot be, the other way around.

PART TWENTY-FIVE

MAE DAY

"...of all the gin joints in all the world..."

U.S. Highway 12 is the vintage road between St. Paul, Minnesota and Madison, Wisconsin. I-94 is the quicker, more modern route. One Tuesday morning in 2002, I the road less travelled took. I was on a down and back sales call; about a ten-hour day - so it didn't make much sense to add time, but I prefer glimpses at the past from old trunk highways. Plus, an early morning drive into western Wisconsin presents a marvelous sunrise vista that crowns miniature mountains of limestone that were cut by a million years of rivers taking the paths of least resistance to the Mississippi.

About a half hour from my destination, at the intersection of Highway 12 and Kickaboo Road, I passed a two-story building of white clapboard siding trimmed in black that stood by itself and invited passersby with its charm.

The front of the building doesn't have a sign, per se, just a wonderful throw-back logo above the front porch that looked like it was taken from a baseball jersey. It featured the word 'Missouri' in cursive writing underlined by a wide tale off the 'i' encasing the word 'Tavern'.

As a guy with a Missouri gal for a wife, a grandfather from the Show-Me state, and a penchant for holes-in-the-wall, I knew I'd be stopping on my return. And I did.

The Missouri Tavern was in decent shape but a bit rough around the edges; there wasn't a car in the lot. I thought it might be out-of-business closed, but soon discovered else-wise.

Alice's looking glass had nothing on that screen door as it slapped shut behind me and I entered an otherworldly space. It looked like someone's 1960s living room that happened to have a pool table. There was an old-timey sofa, comfy chairs, coffee tables, a wood-burning stove to the left, and an upright piano to the right of a well-seasoned mahogany bar about 30 feet long.

There wasn't a soul in the joint and I still wasn't sure if it was open for business or a static display; but I hopefully nestled up to the bar for what would turn into one of the most sanguine experiences of my life.

Floorboards creaked as the bartender approached. *Must live upstairs*, I thought, and was right. I was already forming an image of the grizzled veteran bartender with a pot belly stressing the buttons on a flannel shirt. The only part I got right was 'veteran'.

Through the door stepped Mae Mefford, a 97-year-old, white-haired woman who would have blended into a photo with my aunts Alice, Lena, and Helen down on the farm. Mae and her husband, Al, opened the tavern, gas station, and general store in 1940. Al passed in '64 and Mae never got around to leaving.

"Good afternoon, young man," she said. I was 41 at the time. Most of us have special regard for near-centenarians; Mae's aura far exceeded the norm and was palpable.

I recalled a line from my favorite John Milton sonnet, *"... love, sweetness, goodness, in her person shin'd..."* and it did in

Mae, along with a lingering hint of melancholy left over from the difficult years. I had an instant, yet quizzical admiration for her. How on earth did she get to this place?

Mae wondered the same of me as she served a long-neck Miller High Life. I had shared my Missouri ties and asked if I should be drinking St. Louis's Budweiser, or the official beverage of Wisconsin.

"Well," she said, "I'm from South Dakota, been here since the late '30s, and I don't drink."

"Highlife it is," I replied, then followed with the obvious question, "So how does this place come to be named for Missouri?"

She told me of her husband, "Missouri Al" Mefford, being from St. Louis, then seamlessly flowed into life reflections of good times, hard times, and how in the end they all come together as one. The World War years started within months of their opening. Sacrifice was the norm, and rationing of gas, metal, meat, and sugar, was everywhere – as was bootlegging. Everyone knew a casualty, and everyone was scared in some way, but the war brought the everyones together.

In '63, when John Kennedy was assassinated, people started to change. When Al passed in '64, Mae had to change, and by 1968, the whole country was changed; including the way people drove from Milwaukee, Chicago, and Madison to the Twin Cities, the Mayo, or the Black Hills. The Interstate Highway had arrived in Dane County, Wisconsin and almost erased the corner of Hwy 12 and Kickaboo Road.

Little did Mae know that her world of horse-and-buggy, then horseless carriage, would evolve to become her bread-and-butter, then the bane of her existence. Little did she know that she would watch humanity touch the moon, and the hand-written word become a novelty; that she would see Morse Code and the telephone party line give way to one little gizmo that could talk to outer space... all in one lifetime.

Mae, with Jesus by her side, worked through it all. The scrubbing, stitching, baking, and slinging beers blended into a recipe for a well-lived and fully earned life.

To this day I wish I'd been taking notes, and it crossed my mind at one point to go out to the truck for pen and paper, but I decided it better to leave the spontaneity alone, to take in the experience as a befriended traveler rather than feature writer; to live the moment like some trapper who happened to hit it off with Pig's Eye Parrant back when his trading post was the only White man's joint in what is now St. Paul, Minnesota.

The lack of written notes couldn't detract from the soft grit and ageless wisdom of this extraordinary woman who would seem completely out of place at any other bar in the world but defined the character of this one.

"Great old piano," I said at one point in the conversation, "does it get any use?"

"All the time," she smiled. "I'll play you a tune."

"Oh, gosh," I said, having noted the "No Profanity" sign above the bar and fully sensing she meant it, "That would be great."

Mae was locally famous for closing early if patrons got vulgar and praised for times when she played hymns on the piano over those who were cussing... "to take them to a higher place," she'd say.

"What do you like?" Mae asked.

"Well, I'm kind of a Mozart guy," I said with more hope than pretention – by this time, there was nothing about Mae that would have surprised me. She had captured my heart as one who was about as close as you could get to being a living, breathing illustration of God's intended human condition.

"Let's see what we can do," she said after taking a seat. She didn't play Mozart. We had talked of the importance of faith and family, and I may be inventing memories, but I swear she intuitively knew a couple of my favorite hymns.

She wanted to keep playing. "What else?"

I wracked my brain but was buried by a billion options, then it struck me, and I asked in obvious revelation, "Hey, what was that tune Harry Truman made famous? I think he played it on the news reels."

"The Missouri Waltz."

"Of course."

What a glorious moment in time, I thought as I listened. The live music, delivered with sweet joy, was an unexpected pleasure within an unexpected pleasure. After only two beers, I felt inebriated. I was thankful for the unique and wonderful gift of a private audience with one of God's most sincere works of art; I thanked Him again for keeping it private. If another patron had walked in, the atmosphere would have burst like a cartoon bubble and drifted away in little white puffs.

Mae told me of how she taught herself to play during a spell when a loved one – her sister, perhaps – had an extended illness. I assumed this was when she was a young woman and Al bought her a piano to honor a long-time love of music. Not so. I don't recall the year, but she was old enough to receive retirement checks at the time.

"You're never too old," she said. "I had quite a bit on my mind and the piano helped out."

We covered a lot of territory in two and a half hours. She was as good a listener as she was storyteller. She asked thoughtful questions, made the experience a mutual discovery, and seemed to absorb as much as she shared. Her spirit remains forever with me after our chance, one-time meeting.

When it was finally time to leave, Mae came around the bar and gave me a hug. I'd recently lost a grandmother who half-raised me, and the closest tie to my mother, Aunty Sis – within a week of each other.

Leaving Mae had a familiar feel.

As I slowly strode across the wood-planked floor with my back to the bar, she slid over to the piano and bade me farewell with one more round of the Missouri Waltz from a dusty old piano, in an unlikely tavern, alongside the road less travelled.

Writer's Note:
Mae passed in November of 2005 after 101 years of fine tuning a soul. The owners of the Tavern still honor her with a fundraiser for a local scholarship, and an annual event: MaeFest, held each Fall.

PART TWENTY-SIX

FAMOUS

"Let's roll."

My wife, Mary Beth, was born in Iowa and has deep family history there. Her mother is from Waterloo, and the grandmother after whom we named our daughter, Mary Murphy, is from Sioux City. Mary Beth's father, Joe, was from Iowa, too. The state produced a disproportionate number of A-List and influential people during America's Industrial Age; among them, John Wayne, Donna Reed, George Washington Carver, Johnny Carson, Herbert Hoover, and Jerry Mathers as The Beaver.

Most Millennials looking at that list would probably give it a 'who, wha..?" and that's understandable. Few Americans recognize Al Jolson, who was once "The World's Greatest Entertainer," and whose peak fame would make Taylor Swift and Kanye look like pikers.

Superstar recognition lasts about a generation and a half – celebrity status even less. If I were to mention Doris Day, Walter Cronkite, Billie Holiday, or Louis Prima to my daughter, she'd ask if they were friends from high school or college. If not for Christmas, Nat King Cole would be little known, and even the Beatles – the one-time definition of universal superstardom – are 'kinda' recognized and usually regarded with a shrug of indifference by the young.

Fads have even less staying power. Rocks have ceased to be domesticated and returned to their sedentary pasts. Collectibles like Beanie Babies and baseball cards that people once treasured like the vases of Ming, went the way of Enron stock. Greasers, sock-hops, disco, and urban cowboys came and went just as surely as the Flappers and Charlestons of the Roarin' 20s.

Most Boomers couldn't identify Norman Borlaug of Cresco, IA, a Nobel Prize winner who revolutionized agriculture and the feeding of the world, or the five Sullivan brothers of Waterloo who perished aboard the USS Juneau in WWII and forever changed US Military policy.

Even fewer people will recognize another, hardly famous, yet influential five-pack of brothers from about an hour north of the Sullivans.

The Burnett boys, Jack, Bill, Pat, Tom, and Joe are all included on the Veteran's Memorial in a downtown Mason City Park, across the street from the Frank Lloyd Wright hotel and just a few miles from where Buddy Holly and "the music" died.

The brothers made significant contributions in military service, education, and public policy. All Hollywood handsome, the boys were outdoorsmen who loved cigars and Manhattans – usually, but not always - in conservative moderation.

They were Depression-era, whale-bone-tough; a condition magnified by raising them, from birth to military enlistment, on top of each other in an 850 sq. ft. home not far from the Holy Family parish that would become an integral part of their upbringing and life perspectives. These brothers – along with the women and the family trees into which they married — would leave a poignant stamp on human history's timeline.

Jack, the oldest, was a Lt. Colonel in the Air force who island-hopped the Pacific, flew on to Korea and Vietnam, then to an attaché position in New Zealand where he once hosted President Lyndon Johnson. In the Pacific he was known by airplane mechanics to return from low-level attacks with foliage in his landing gear. Prior to combat, Jack left Great Lakes Air Base in Chicago on a training mission and decided to implement a different flight plan than the one "suggested" by the trainers; he flew the plane to Mason City to see his mother, Margaret. He got socked in by fog in Mason City, but somehow talked his way out of a court-martial.

Bill, a one-time college football player, was the most rugged. He and his saintly wife Kay raised six boys of their own. In a kinder-gentler moment, Bill coined the phrase "soft clothes" to describe the comfortable attire one would slip into as the day unwinds.

Bill's son, Tim, fit the rugged Burnett mold and recounted a story wherein he and some buddies had a few beers at a Wyoming rodeo and decided to queue up and pay $5 to be amateur bull riders. Tim said they knew it wouldn't go well when, as they stood trapped in a cattle chute, the announcer boomed out to the crowd, "Brrrring on the Christians!"

Pat was the brother most likely to become a priest and studied to do so. The calling was revoked by a faithless misunderstanding of epilepsy. His son, Chuck, built his own altar, and became a prominent real estate agent on the Dakota side of Sioux City where he hunts birds when he isn't spinning yarns on the way to a home sale.

Mary Beth's dad, Joe, was the youngest, and while none of the Burnett boys lacked street smarts, a childhood of shutting up and listening made him very savvy, and an excellent gambler. His finesse wasn't always appreciated in the military complex, and Joe claimed to be the only soldier in the Korean Conflict who wasn't asked to re-enlist. His insights led to a top spot at Minnesota Mining and Manufacturing, 3M, where he lobbied legislatures across the country to transform transportation with reflective highway stripes and signs. Their efforts led to hundreds of thousands of saved lives throughout the nation, then the world.

The longest survivor of the boys was 93-year-old Tom, who passed in February of 2023. He was a larger-than-life personality with a big voice that could fill a room with charm. He was a consummate storyteller who taught high school in classrooms where kids knew who was in charge. Tom was a favorite at the Minnesota Veterans home, a place where old soldiers go... to never die.

From these boys who became influential men - and just up the road from the notable Iowans - did their ultimate legacy emerge in a remarkable level of fame; one that simultaneously represents the best and the worst paths to household name status.

On September 11, 2001, Joe made a most unexpected phone call to ask how I was doing.

"Just fine, Joe," I replied, "with the exception that it's been one of the most overwhelming days of my life."

"Well, Mike... it's about to get more so... Tom Junior was on Flight 93."

We both sat in a silent pause for a time, then I said. "As you might expect, Mary Beth is still at work and can't be interrupted. I'll have her call the minute she walks in."

Mary Beth was an airline employee on 9/11, and it was an *all-hands-on-deck* day in that industry.

"Thank you. Give the girls a hug for us," Joe concluded.

Thomas Burnett Jr. of Bloomington, Minnesota: son, nephew, and cousin, joined a group of American heroes in the sky, then a field in Pennsylvania, to become one of the distinguished citizen soldiers of Flight 93. They were combatants in a seemingly endless struggle that brings worldviews together in the most destructive way. The selfless sacrifice by people who treasure liberty tragically emerged in New York, Washington DC, and over Pennsylvania where the words "Let's Roll," entered American lexicon along with declarations like, *I have not yet begun to fight*, and *I regret that I have but one life to give for my country.*

Ten years after that fateful day in September, I would hear the most awe-inspiring sound of my life – silence. The Burnett family, mother Bev, father Tom Sr., sisters Martha, and Mary Margaret – their spouses and children – were invited to TCF Bank stadium for a 9/11 remembrance during halftime at a Minnesota Gophers football game. The family invited cousin Mary Beth along with me and our daughter, Murphy, to join them at the tribute.

As our group of about a dozen faced the home crowd from midfield, the Public Address announcer reminded us of how Tom Burnett, Todd Beamer, Mark Bingham, Jeremy Glick, Sandra Bradshaw and others, exhibited supreme courage that concluded with the ultimate sacrifice on behalf of their families and the principles of Individual Liberty.

The thrill of a standing ovation from thousands must be exhilarating. On this day I witnessed, and the family experienced, something far more powerful.

A photo of Tom Jr. filled the jumbo screen behind us and there was not a single sound to be heard in that stadium. The college kids stopped being fanatics, the cooks set down their tongs, and the hawkers stopped hawking. There was no song in the band.

The tribute had nothing to do with me, but because I was standing with them, I could physically feel the emotion that flowed tenderly down from the highest rows of the stadium as tens of thousands of people – in sixty seconds of utter solemn silence – honored the sacrifices made by people I love, people who wished they'd never seen such distinction, and never had such fame.

From Iowa to Islamabad, interesting, influential, infamous, and inspirational personalities emerge in mere moments to dominate local, regional, and worldwide stages.

And yet, time belongs to no one. Whether by determined desire or heroic conclusion, fame is always fleeting.

PART TWENTY-SEVEN

THE CONFIDENT SHEPARD

I got my inheritance on a Target Gift Card. Pop's essence and net worth was captured on a magnetic strip, encased in plastic, and swiped into a digital cloud within two weeks of his passing. Remember, man, that you are bytes, and to bytes you shall return.

I received the card at a picnic out in the hardwood hills of a big park just south of Saint Paul. One well-organized sister amassed his remaining resources – that included a $256 insurance payout – and decided that the $315 estate could be most easily divided with three $15 gift cards to each of seven siblings.

The trees cut the heat that August day, and guided breezes to blow memories around in little eddies among the picnickers.

For the first time in years, the Marines of the Korean Conflict weren't at the annual barbecue. Dad had died two weeks before, and Uncle Lefty was at home gathering peace and courage for his final days.

The little brothers and sisters of 'The Greatest Generation' had sewn their seeds and laid the foundations for a New Age, in a New Century, in a New Millennium. The evidence was scattered throughout the park – from kids to great grandkids who were cooking ribs, tossing bean bags, and staring at cell phones.

Pop's generation was born into the dusty desperation of the Great Depression. His family and neighbors grubbed, begged, and picked coal from railroad tracks to heat their homes. They blasted through the global wars of the 20th Century, then wrenched, and hammered, and innovated their way through the smoke, oily grime, and meat & potatoes of the Industrial Age.

The fruit of their labor is a transitional and contradicting blend of clean coal, silicon, saturated fats, and artificial intelligence known as the Technology Age.

My father's generation has an ageless tale; one of greed, arrogance, denial, and never-ending expansion and contraction. It's the story of pathetic pursuits for money, materialism, and pseudo-sophistication – of idolizing one-dimensional talents, blind bigotry, and escaping into a glass screen to distract one's mind from what it should really be doing.

But as I said, it's an ageless tale, so it's also a beautiful story of love and sacrifice, forgiveness, and redemption.

We scheduled Dad's memorial a couple of weeks after his passing to give out-of-towners time to make plans to attend a weekend reunion that included the annual family barbecue.

I really wanted to write Pop's eulogy but knew my family well enough to not self-nominate. Plus, our oldest sister, Chell, was the unmistakable matriarch of the family and had far more experience with important speaking engagements. I expected to silently defer, then be proud and weepy at her wonderful sentiments.

I was surprised when, during a conference-call regarding the subject, Chell said, "I think Mike should do it." I acted like I was a last resort, but my siblings all knew I was full of crap when I said, "well, if nobody else wants to…" The moment was a perfect representation of Chell's selfless nature.

I spent almost every free hour for the next ten days locked in our man-cave garage working on the piece. I'd look up at the flag that my father's father received for his service in World War I, and at a shadow box of memorabilia from Pop's service in Korea: it had a large Marine Corps emblem behind his dress cap, a replica of the Tun Tavern, and a team-signed soccer ball from his days at the Naval Academy where he was an award-winning goaltender.

Our garage, nicknamed 'The Pond,' had an atmosphere like a seasoned country tavern and was a common gathering place for family, friends, neighbors, and 'miscreants' as one of the regulars called us.

The walls were plastered with tidbits that made it a life-long storyboard for me: Grandad Aleshire's 1930s baseball uniform from his barnstorming days with Dizzy Dean, religious remembrances of dearly departed, vintage banners, and trophies from long-forgotten championships. There were year-round Christmas lights in the rafters, and patriotic cardboard bunting hanging from the trusses. Historic black and white photos of Abe and George, Einstein, Churchill, Mark Twain and Frederick Douglass were displayed as well – along with a tribute to the women of WWII and the storming of Omaha beach.

The garage was the ideal setting to think about the man who taught me to think.

After several drafts, I finally settled on one and sent it to Chell with a plea, "I'm so close to this now, I have no idea if it does the job or is a rambling mess."

"I've never been so proud of you, Mike," was her response.

I shivered and sighed in relief. There was, however, one more huge hurdle to overcome: how on earth could I deliver the words without becoming a puddle of emotion that made the whole room more uncomfortable than the sniveling son?

Lots of practice would help, but I suspected it wouldn't be quite enough. I turned to faith and was inspired to write the letters JMJ atop the script - for Jesus, Mary, and Joseph - that I could turn to for comfort. That thought inspired another.

John and Karen were friends at church. Karen passed away suddenly while eight and a half months pregnant. John lost his wife and baby as he lay sleeping beside them. He also delivered their eulogies with superhuman grace and poise. I added his initials to the top of the page - and with their help - made it through my father's eulogy with only a few slight pauses.

Eulogy of Rex Levering Pickett Jr. (delivered 8/10/2013)

"A pessimist sees the difficulty in every opportunity, an optimist the opportunity in every difficulty."

– Winston Churchill

Two weeks ago, Rex Pickett was not perfect, but today he is. I love that about eulogies. They're testaments to forgiveness… to the hope and faith within each one of us.

A couple of months ago at Dad's birthday celebration, Joanne Tierney reminded us that – even among people raised during the Great Depression – Dad had a unique ability to emerge from the dark side of tragedy with a fresh perspective and encouraging word. Those times taught him that success and happiness are found in creation, not consumption.

This hardscrabble Marine, turned soft grandpa, was no stranger to tragedy. Between 1970 and '76, he lost his home to fire, his wife to cancer, and his business to economics – not to mention a couple of cars to teenagers. At 46 years old, he started life over with nothing but debt and hungry mouths to feed. He stumbled, got up, and dusted himself off.

When he was 77, Dad had a stroke that left him on the floor for two days. Doctors informed us he might make it through the night, but not the next day. Two years later, he beat me at golf. Medical professionals called it the most remarkable and courageous stroke recovery they'd ever seen… I called it a lucky putt…

So, Dad was no stranger to pain. I believe one of the reasons he was so beloved was his unique brand of compassion. He knew that empathy could only go so far. So rather than affirm, and reaffirm, an unfortunate condition, he'd start a rally… with a story… or a poem. Pity was not in his lexicon. To quote Dad, "Pity? What the hell for? There's no inherent value in pity."

His lectures were epic. As a matter of fact, he missed them so much after the kids were gone that he took to lecturing everyone in this room with his essays and poems. Dad's written words, however, took on a different tone. Barking sermons became soft, sincere, parables of life. His writing is packed with the wisdom of indisputable truths. Instructive words like honesty, courage, hard work, and principles, are balanced with encouraging words like imagine, nourish, celebrate, love, and peace.

Dad was a confirmed conservative, part Eisenhower, part Reagan, part Kennedy and Truman. He knew that real conservatives give more than they receive, that they defend and protect the vulnerable and – regardless of bad luck, bad weather, or gross injustice – it is the responsibility of the individual to be their own solution.

These convictions didn't exclude charity or work on behalf of others. Mom once said to Dad, "Well, Pickett, I guess we're never gonna be rich. We'll end up giving it all away before we ever get there."

He and Mom went 'Green' fifty years before anyone ever heard of a carbon footprint. They were chairs of the Natural Resources Committee in Bloomington (MN) in the early '60s and instrumental to preserving the flood plains, watersheds, and aquifers of the Minnesota River Valley from Saint Paul to LeSeuer.

They were also champions of youth activities and facilities. If you ever played a hockey game in St. Louis Park or at the Bloomington Ice Gardens, you could give partial thanks to Dad. If you attended a BAC football game in Burnsville between 1969 and '75, there's a strong chance you were treated to coffee and doughnuts from Pickett's restaurant.

We've all seen The Most Interesting Man in the World television commercials. Dad's life was not as funny, or clever, but it shared the ironic twists. He was strong in weakness, powerful in frailty, and arrogant in humility... he was a pragmatic sentimentalist. Dad was not a great man in the sense that he discovered a cure for cancer; he was a great person because he could soothe the effects of cancer in another. He was a constant, an inspiration, and a giver of hope.

The Latin origin of the word 'confidence' is con-fides, 'con' meaning 'with', 'fides' meaning 'faith'. Confidence; "with faith."

We too often associate confidence with superiority, or to a competition that awards spoils to the victor. The truly confident person is a shepherd; one who shoulders responsibility, leads by example, and shares success with the entire flock.

Rex Pickett was the confident shepherd.

PART TWENTY-EIGHT

EMIGRATIONS

My feet sank into the frosty grass as I stood overlooking the burial site of Jonas and Mary Aleshire at Mt. Pleasant cemetery in Hancock County, Illinois. The old Methodist church was gone, but the perpetual care remained – for now, at least.

It was Christmas Eve day, and the morning sun was chasing frost to hide behind pillars of granite that marked the final resting places for one of many tribes which have worked their way across the rolling hills and winding creeks of North America's central plains.

Tribes come and go from places like Hancock County by instinct, inspiration, and appropriation. Without Jonas and Mary, I never would have been there – or anywhere, for that matter.

As my feet sank and my heart reflected, I was thankful the ground beneath the frost wasn't frozen. I'd made the trek down from Minnesota to mom's ancestral home to bury our beloved Francis, 'the dog they named a Pope after.' Francis obviously wasn't Methodist and would be interred a few miles away at my favorite place on earth, a hillside of wild prairie growth and clay just above Little Creek, where we swam and picked berries in the springtimes of youth; a stone's throw from where I proposed everlasting unity to my wife, and fifty yards from the old stagecoach line that carried Abraham Lincoln on his presidential campaign.

Jonas Aleshire, my great-great-great grandfather, was a member of the Virginia State House and a lead engineer on what became the Robert E. Lee Highway; a road that connects Washington DC with points west. Mary was his wife. They migrated to Illinois in 1852.

Jonas' father, John Conreid Aleshire of "The Old Dominion" - Virginia - was the kind of ancestor who reminds one of how shallow gene pools can get. John crossed the Delaware to fight at Trenton, Princeton, and Yorktown with a friend and local land surveyor named George, who took on temp jobs as Commanding General of the Continental Army, then President of the United States.

George and John were among a group of prominent colonists who "pledged their lives, fortunes, and sacred honor" to the cause of individual liberty. The pledge had some significant asterisks but was a major stepping-stone toward the realization of self-evident truths. It remains a work-in-progress.

John Aleshire outlived his friend by 48 years and was one of the oldest survivors of the American Revolution. The *Philadelphia Courier* eulogized him in a flamboyant newspaper article, (1847) titled, The Relic of '76:

"...The thunder of British cannon was no terror to him. Noble was his resolve! And how noble verified! ... near to the side of the father of his country, he stood before Yorktown with eyes swimming in tears of joy, he beheld the country's flag wave in triumph over the ramparts of the

enemy… a gallant spirit, a pious and respected man with brightest hopes of a happy immortality."

I stumbled across a copy of the article in some of Gram's family stuff and ran with the genealogical patriotism for a while. The World Wide Web had just opened up in the mid 1990s and turned family ties into a hobby shop version of the human genome project.

I dug into mom's Aleshires, and dad's Picketts, then LaBontes, Paynes, Burtons, and Owens. I had the family of Louisa Theodosia Wylie queued up when it dawned on me that for every generation I reached back, I could only take one of four forks in the road, and the available data was quickly consuming the two bytes of storage that came with my brand-new computer and Internet subscription to 'Prodigy.'

I copped out on my great great grandmothers and did what most people do – followed the surnames of the fathers. If one were to tell the immediate family's history from the narrow perspective of our mom and dad, then their dads, and dads, and dads; it would be a mirror of the Western European version of the consummate American Experience. That is, as grandad Aleshire used to say, "if you leave out the pirates, drunks, and horse thieves."

Back on the frosty grass of Mt. Pleasant Cemetery, I wondered about Mary – what she was like. I supposed she was like many women of her day, nearly anonymous to noble eulogies, but the unmistakable weavers of life's fabric. The weaving is heroic, and perhaps the most crucial function of any culture, but, like mortar in a brick building, lacks the sensation preferred in historic remembrance.

The weaving heroines would get a cameo here and there within the tributes to their men; as was the case in "The Relic of

'76." Turns out, without his sister, John Aleshire wouldn't have been weeping with Washington at Yorktown – or anywhere, for that matter. Catherine, or Elizabeth, or Margaret – one of the three – saved John's life.

In January of 1756, John was a baby in a cradle in a homestead on the 'extreme boundaries' of the colonies. Native Americans - whose ancestors had been hunting the property for multiple millennia - showed up to execute a quitclaim of the deed, and anyone who stuck around to challenge its validity.

The family hurried off to seek counsel at a local fort, and in the process, left young John behind. The unacceptable oversight led to the following passage in John's noble eulogy: *"…one sister returned determined to peril her life for his safety, and cautiously approaching the house, entered through the window, succeeded in getting her infant brother in her arms, and bore him in triumph back to the fort."*

As I said – one of the three.

I've met and been cultivated by too many of Mary's agrarian descendants to think of her as subordinate. I witnessed too many selfless partnerships, too much sacrifice and forgiveness to issue judgments based on past media coverage. To me, the women and men are inseparable. I read the chronicles and feel the spirits.

I feel historic, gentle, and intrepid power in my sisters, cousins, and aunts Barbara, Elizabeth, Dorothy, and adopted aunty Beth. I felt it in all the women who nurtured, tutored, and intimidated me: mom and her sister Eileen, great 'grandma Corny', great-great aunts Edithe and Lorraine, grandmothers Eula Juanita and Beulah Cornelia, great aunts Alice, Lena, Helen, Joyce, Flevvy, and even in Diane, who left the family in a separation of faith.

Old newspaper articles are fine for research, but enduring culture lives in storytelling families, and the passions of those who seek to remain attached to preceding spirits. My greatest pain and privilege is that so many families have broken chains of oral history while I got to soak up a million stories that attached me to immigrants and pioneers – to the pious, reckless, callous, and selfless.

One matriarch saved a kid from a fire and died in the process. One patriarch got hit by a train, and another - Jonas' son, Douglas - rode a train car to the bottom of a gorge in the once-famous Gasconade trestle collapse of 1855. Without Doug's incredible good fortune, I never would have heard or told a single tale.

In 2012, I took Pop on a bucket-list visit to his grandparents' farm in New London, Missouri where he pointed out a ravine next to a country road where his great-grandparents hid runaway slaves of broken chains to await a carriage in the night that would take them to freedom. Not long before, those same ancestors had been owners of the people and their chains.

The Aleshire and Pickett family stories are remarkably parallel and became officially related by marriage in 1952 – the centennial of Jonas and Mary's move west. Mom and Pop met in Georgetown near DC, about 90 miles from their great grandparents' farms in Virginia – about the same distance that separated the two families' Manifestly Destined farms in the Midwest. It's as if our parents' marriage was a pre-arranged clause in the 'Manifest' to reunite the Shenandoah families.

The Picketts from Ol' Virginia also crossed the Delaware and froze at Valley Forge. They too, were buddies with George and wept at Yorktown. Four score and seven years later they all would live and die in a house they divided together, against itself, in a not-so Civil War.

Mom's Aleshires went Union, Pop's Picketts went Confederate, until that couple in Missouri succumbed to inalienable truths, and laid underground rails with hopes of forgiveness.

Just down the road from the Show-Me-State Picketts was a family named Clemens whose Twain would spend a lifetime telling all our stories about the triumphs and hypocrisies of the Industrial Age in America.

Long before they had seen the central plains, the Aleshires were Germans named Eldsheidt from the Rhine Valley who set off in 1750 to help anglicize a seemingly open continent. The Picketts arrived in the New World a full century before. They were French Picquetts who started their anglicizing in 1066.

Storytelling has it that Grandpa Picquett (literally meaning, 'long lance') was the armor bearer, or wing man, for the Duke of Normandy and eventual King of England – William the Conqueror – at the battle of Hastings.

After a few hundred years in service to Kings and Queens, the anglicizers abandoned their great British land grabs for the much larger and greener pastures of North America.

Unfortunately, the opportunism of fleeing oppression to becoming an oppressor is not unique to anyone's ancestors. As Grandad used to say, "Gettin' powerful has a way of bringin' out the worst in people. Makes 'em self-righteous. We always get humbled," he'd say, "either by God, or an ass-whoopin'."

Our Francis was naturally humble and had no timeline for interment, so I walked around the cemetery to read names and remember what stories I could before making my way back to Jonas and Mary. Despite local prominence, they saw the coming storm of war and left the Shenandoah Valley in search of peace.

By 1859, as the Aleshires were doing their part for Manifest Destiny, Charles Darwin was simultaneously working on the genealogy of every fork in every tree, of every creature ever on earth – without a Prodigy subscription. He called it "Origin of Species" and it sent humanity on a truth-quest through a scientific and philosophical labyrinth.

I pondered the quests of Aleshires and Picketts during a pilgrimage to Virginia when Mary Beth took me to Shenandoah for my 40th birthday. We hiked into a forgotten field of The Old Dominion to find the headstones of John Conreid Aleshire and his wife, Susanna Pangle, in a cemetery that was just about out of perpetual care.

I hauled a jug of moonshine and the soundtrack to Ken Burns 'Civil War' up a hill above the Jordan Hollow Inn one starry night and sat beneath infinite galaxies to behold the valley and contemplate the origins.

Without a billion variables aligning with the stars, I never would have been there.

We're an army on a perpetual march, an armada of ships endlessly sailing *with brightest hopes of a happy immortality.* There is, however, no fossil in a hidden cave, no secret in the ocean's depth, and no apex of artificial intelligence to reveal the missing link to our origins and eternal truths.

The link isn't even missing; it lies within... patiently waiting for the arrogance to evolve and become one with the wisdom of all ages.

PART TWENTY-NINE

LOVE CARRIES THE DAY

It has been said that bitter trials are often blessings in disguise. Like most of us, I know this to be true. As previously stated, a variety of circumstances sent me to eleven schools between kindergarten and college.

Constant childhood upheaval offered its trials; like the time in third grade at Shawnee Elementary in Lima, Ohio when Carl Umbaugh tripped me - the transplanted Gopher - as I walked to the front of the class to introduce myself to a room full of Buckeyes. Blessings, on the other hand, include a lifetime collection of relationships that far exceed the worthiness of any one person.

The groups of friends from different phases of the journey began with my very first buddy in the world, Jimmy Brinkhaus, who still lives near several friends within a block of our early '60s home in Bloomington, Minnesota.

Rosemount High gave me a handful of brothers along with a graduating class that gathers in a pole barn every five years with renewed thankfulness.

Augsburg College delivered a priceless Lutheran brotherhood of multiple faiths and creeds that began with sophomoric antics and has never stopped evolving, and the parishioners of Nativity of Our Lord Church and Men's Club have been a network of unwavering faith and camaraderie for what is now a majority of my life.

I'm thankful for an arm's length connection to the West 7th Boys Club of St. Paul – a group of men and women who are 10-15 years older but let me hang around like a little brother they got tired of ditching.

Then there's the largest of my groups – numerically, at least – a gang of grade school and junior high pals and gals from Burnsville known as 'The Dogs' who relate to each other like first cousins in a three-legged race at a rural picnic.

Each faction, in their moment, is equally precious to me. To identify a favorite group – let alone individual – would be like trying to choose the best steak from a herd of cattle on a Kansas prairie.

On the evening of December 30, 2018, my cell phone started chirping a ding-ding-ding sequence that usually meant one of the text-happy Men's Club guys had found an inane tidbit on social media, or that they were looking for a garage in which to watch a ballgame. I was in a garage wrenching on a car... OK, I was holding the flashlight for a neighbor who had put himself through college as a mechanic, never lost the knack or desire, and was wrenching on a car.

A glance at my phone revealed an ominous foreshadow. It was The Dogs. For decades, our core bonding device was a softball team. On December 30, 2018, The Dogs leadoff man was battling both Parkinson's and cancer, our coach-figure – who always, unselfishly batted last – was in his seventh year of pancreatic cancer, and our intellectual sage was physically confined by ALS to voice-activated software and a hulking contraption that looked more like the Mars Rover than a wheelchair.

It had been five days since burying our beloved dog, Francis, and Mary Beth and I had begun to prepare our home of 21 years for sale. Adapting was hardly a foreign condition, but these days were different. In addition to personal lifestyle adjustment, the American worldview was in rapid transformation. Baby Boomers had aged to Senior status and Postwar expansion and discovery was becoming the stuff of legend rather than a way of life. Our parents, aunts, uncles, and mentors were passing on a near-daily basis, and our generation had begun the practice of sharing health maladies before talking about our children.

My heart was saddened with certainty before I returned a single call to one of The Dogs; the sadness was accurate, but not at all for what I could anticipate.

One cannot easily identify a favorite group of friends, but a group of friends can reach consensus of special distinction – especially among couples. Tim and Kim (Bowser) O'Brien were the poster couple of The Dogs and living stereotypes of inspiration. Hard-working, churchgoing, responsible, giving, and slow-to-anger.

Both had ever-ready smiles. He was a 35-year employee at the peak of his career who always invested wisely. She, a one-time model with a tender sweetness who worked in the kitchen of a local grade school. They were generous together. They birthed, and adopted, and raised two great kids, and – even in their late 50s – looked like a pose for the top of a wedding cake. We all knew these youthful-looking, faith-filled anchors would be among the last of our clan. We all knew that our collective presence here on earth would be closed out with a level of Grace that, among us, only Kim and Tim possessed.

The great joys and gifts of life, however, are always brought to universal balance. Sometimes with sudden tragedy and great mystery - as was the case with the O'Briens.

New Year's weekend was upon us, and the couple had shared an evening meal with family during a retreat to a restaurant in the backwoods of Wisconsin. They decided to "take the long road home" on their snowmobile to meet back at the cabin. Along the way, beneath a gorgeous, starlit winter night, God took them home, together, through an opening of water beneath the machine.

The bitterness of trial comes in many forms and degrees. Self-imposed pain, unfortunate coincidence, inevitable conclusion. The passing – in a moment – of Tim and Kim, two people who had so much, and shared so much, was incomprehensible to all who loved them. It was easy to appreciate and applaud the lives they had built together, but impossible to envy. They were too kind and thankful to apply any negative connotation.

The church was filled with universal dismay during remembrances. Grief is difficult to process when one loses an aged grandparent. On this day, reconciliation of such a significant and abrupt loss felt like an appointment to be made in the distant future.

There was a moment however, of raw wisdom and hard faith that brought into perspective the incalculable value of family and longtime friendships - the priest instructed us to look around the room at the outpouring of unanimous love.

"Death does not rule today," he said, "Love carries this day."

And so it does each day. In friendship, joy, in family, and in bitter trial.

PART THIRTY

NOT ALWAYS TO THE SWIFT

Ecclesiastes 9:11 reminds us that "...the race is not always to the swift, nor the battle to the strong..." Maybe not, but according to Damon Runyon, "but that's the way to bet."

I lived a parable and turned Damon Runyon's wisdom on its ear one July day while Mary Beth and our friends, Sue and Steve, were enjoying the Sport of Kings at Canterbury Park in Shakopee, MN.

I have my wife's father, Joe Burnett, to thank for her appreciation of horse tracks. The Burnetts got thoroughbred racing in their blood after he put himself through college at Arizona State with the GI Bill and work at the newly opened Turf Paradise in the late 1950s. He had keen instincts for human behavior combined with a take-it-or-leave-it worldview that made him an excellent gambler. His son, Tom, follows in his footsteps, but Joe taught me only one thing about gambling: I'm lousy at it.

"I love the thrill of it, but don't bet very much,' I once said to him, "I'm not very good."

"I know," he said, "you're too curious."

I had never gambled with Joe.

With horse racing a part of the family heritage, Mary Beth likes to combine her love of animals with her father's partiality to the pari-mutuel, and I get to go to the track a couple times a year. Canterbury Park enjoys a partnership with the Mdewakanton Sioux Community who operate Mystic Lake Casino just a few miles down the road. The Tribe's large sponsorship of the track increases winners' purses, and the track limits its direct competition with the casino.

Canterbury has several high stakes races per year with purses (prize money) that draw better horses, and more fans. On this particular day, we had seats out in the sun near the finish line and, as the day's promotional race neared, people gathered on the rail for a closer look at the competitors as they entered the track under control of leather straps that would at first guide them, then set them free to run with pure instinct.

The entrants had prepared for this race their entire lives with special diets, secret training sessions, and the hopeful love of their owners.

I'm actually not half bad at reading a racing form and have picked the Kentucky Derby winner five times in 35 years, which is about 15% and better than most. For this race, I was true to Joe's analysis and my wagering strategy was more emotional than deductive.

Number three in the program was named Ringo. My brother went by that same nickname from the age of two. It was supposed to be just Ring, shortened from Rex Levering Pickett III, but 4-year-old sister Chell entered a room one day, and said, "Hello Mommio, Daddio, and Ringo." Mom and Dad looked at each other and the name stuck.

I owe my brother bolts of hand-me-down cloth, several leftover forts, bicycles, fixed toys, years of adventures, black eyes, skinned knees, and at least a dozen unpaid rents on Boardwalk and Park Place. How could I not bet on number three?

We decided to do an internal bet amongst the group for the big race and Sue collected the money. With the name Ringo on the docket, I didn't need to read the form and was unaware of the significant handicap carried by my selection.

For those not familiar with horse racing handicaps, officials allocate a different weight to be carried by each horse. This evens out their speed and makes for a more compelling betting environment.

It was obvious to everyone that there was no justice in Ringo's handicap that day – it never should have happened. The handlers paraded their entrants for review on the big screen.

"See that?" Sue asked, then thoughtfully added, "You can change your bet if you want."

"Oh, my." I replied and thought for a second. There really was no way for Ringo to overcome that handicap and six other hungry competitors. To be honest, he was a bit obese, too – which is uncommon in a horse track setting.

Nobody had any expectations of a win for Ringo; he was the definition of a hopeless longshot; but I stuck with the 'never change a bet' theory and loyalty to my brother's name; plus he was number three, a sign of the Trinity. "Thanks, but I gotta stay with him," I said.

Steve applauded my allegiance and appreciated the increased odds of winning his bet. He's a bright guy who's long on math and deductive reasoning skills that helped him win three races in a row earlier in the day, including a trifecta that had their trip to the track bought and paid for.

"Good for you, Mike," he said with sincerity, then added, "Sucka…"

As the animals began their charge down the home stretch I, and a lot of folks, felt bad for Ringo. The handicap was so substantial it made his gait different from all the others. He stayed on a steady, determined course in the center of the track but was running last. He boldly, awkwardly drove for the finish line, but simply couldn't compete with the younger, healthier, faster animals.

Then, out of nowhere, a distraction arose at the side of the track. A gate was left open where several owners had gathered to witness the race. First one, then two, then five of the seven sprinters veered off course toward the open gate. It was chaos like I've never seen on a track.

A sixth racer paused long enough for Ringo to take the lead. There were only yards remaining as he battled down the stretch. Number six, Mister Dexter, refocused and was back in the race for a late comeback. His white coat and pink silks were a distinct contrast to Ringo's chestnut and black with Kelly green silks, so it was easy to see exactly how much ground was being regained.

The lead shrunk to a body length… then a half-length… it was gonna be close. Dirt from the track flew up behind him as Ringo dug in with one more dauntless stride then surged across the finish line in triumph.

The crowd roared and exchanged high fives and fist bumps for the lovable underdog as track announcer Paul Allen declared Ringo's victory among the greatest in the history of racing at Canterbury.

We waited around to personally meet the winner and his owners after the fanfare and hoopla settled down. They thanked us for the unwavering support as Ringo beamed with satisfaction at his achievement, and I gladly accepted a photo op for bragging rights on social media.

Everyone else was going with Damon Runyon theory that day, so I was one of few people to bet on Ol' Number 3, but

I didn't cash a big ticket. Three dollars to be exact – one each from Mary Beth, Sue, and Steve.

The promotional feature this day wasn't a high stakes thoroughbred race... It was *Wiener Dogs and Donuts Day*... and Ringo is a 3-legged dachshund who allocated his own handicap in a desperate act of self-preservation that freed him from an animal trap.

The full verse of Ecclesiastes 9:11 states: *"I have seen something else under the sun: The race is not to the swift, or the battle to the strong, nor does food come to the wise, or wealth to the brilliant, or favor to the learned; but time and chance happen to them all,"*

...including a brave little wiener dog named Ringo.

PART THIRTY-ONE

OPENING DAYS

Major League Baseball and I were both born to Bloomington, Minnesota in 1961. We were Twins... but not identical. I'm younger, so I've been a fan since birth, and my life can be divided into memories that have paralleled baseball since the Twins kicked the Minneapolis Millers out of the ball yard once called "an Erector Set in a cornfield," Metropolitan Stadium.

"The Met" was our field of dreams and my oldest memory is there - Bat Day in 1964.

Jimmy Brinkhaus and I - and a few thousand other kids - got new, full-sized Louisville Sluggers compliments of the ball club and Hillerich & Bradsby Co. "Win Twins," was carved on the sweet spot. Unlike the tiny, worthless bats they give away today - with pizza franchise logos - these bats were fully functional and critical to maintaining the game's status as America's pastime.

By midsummer, equipment would be hard to come by in neighborhoods like ours on Beard Avenue, so we'd use anything shaped like a stick to hit anything shaped like a ball – including the head off your little sister's doll.

"Bat Day" bats replaced chunks of lumber that looked like a long rawhide for a dog; they had electrical tape on the handles, and cracks that were *fixed* by pounding a 20# sinker nail through the barrel. There are only two of those 1964 giveaways remaining on earth, and one is listed on eBay for $22.50; it's "used but in good condition," so I know it's not from Beard Avenue.

On April 11, 1961, the world was still being captured in black and white. At Yankee Stadium Marilyn Monroe, Toots Shor, and Joe DiMaggio watched – probably in shock – as Mickey Mantle, Yogi Berra, Whitey Ford, and the Yanks got thumped 6-0 by the Twins in their first game ever.

The dreamers peaked that day. The Twins' one game lead disappeared, then they got swept in a double header on Father's Day – the day I was born –– and the Damn Yankees went on to win the World Series... again.

The Twins ran two minor league teams out of town that year, and the Minneapolis Millers and St. Paul Saints were separate, and not equal, to their big-league parents in the Big Apple. The Giants chucked the Polo Grounds in Washington Heights for the golden hills of San Francisco, and the (trolley) Dodgers left Brooklyn's Flatbush neighborhood and Ebbets Field for Elysian Park at Chaves Ravine in Los Angeles.

The Millers folded, and the Saints went to Omaha.

By 1965, full color had come to Minnesota baseball when Met Stadium hosted both the All-Star game and the World Series with names like Mudcat, Battey, Zoilo, Camilo and the phenom, Tony-O. In the Mid-summer Classic, the American League trailed by five runs early before local favorite Harmon Killebrew tied the game with a two-run bomb in the fifth.

The National Leaguers who left broken hearts in the boroughs did more of the same in a Midwestern cornfield with a one-run victory.

The loss moved the North Star, and Minnesota became the Close-But-No-Cigar state. Sandy Koufax and the Dodgers beat us in the World Series three months later, and there were Twin killings in '69 and '70 by Baltimore in the League Championship. Minnesota's football Vikings claimed their first of four second-place finishes in 1970, and the state's favorite son, Hubert Humphrey, became Vice President in relief after the Kennedy assassination, then presidential runner-up to Nixon in the balloting of '68. On the stage of world politics and confrontation, Minnesotans participated as the U.S. finished second to the Commies in Vietnam.

In the mid '60s, parents and baseball executives picked their battles more carefully; they let kids be kids. Twins' owner Calvin Griffith didn't fix the bent-up corner of a metal fence in left field at Met Stadium where youngsters would drop their bikes, climb over, then crawl under the bleachers to chat through chain link with outfielders like Al Kaline, Roger Maris, or the Twins' Bobby Allison and Tony Oliva - before his knees went bad. Once a year, Pop would take us to sit in seats and eat popcorn from a cone-shaped cardboard cup that turned into a megaphone.

If you couldn't climb a bent fence, watch through a knot hole, or eat popcorn in an actual seat, radio was the way to experience baseball. Back before television corrupted sports with piles of cash that turned folk heroes into false Gods, there were voices that painted the pictures of baseball artistry with phrases like, "Tinkers, to Evers, to Chance," "The Giants win the pennant!" and, "Holy Cow."

Vin Scully was the master of atmosphere and stayed quiet when a roaring crowd was greater than words. If the time was right for description, he'd say things like: "…he's twitching his leg like a horse trying to get rid of an irksome fly…"

The broadcasters were everyone's uncle, some you loved some not – Mel Allen, Ernie Harwell, Harry Caray. Scully's first broadcast featured a man born during the Civil War and the last game he did was played by Millennials.

I claim allegiance to the many voices of baseball and to a team from each circuit: the AL Twins of course, and down at the farm in Illinois, Grandma Eula was a huge fan of Jack Buck and the National League's Cardinals – so I was, too. Stan Musial sat next to her at a lunch counter one time in St. Louis as she waited for Grandad to finish a cattle buy. Gramps was all fired up when he sat down and bragged that he just traded 'hellos' with the Cardinal great.

"Is that who that was?" Gram smugly replied. "He just left that seat. Very nice man."

Pat Aleshire 'Gramps' was no stranger to baseball, or the Cardinals. He played semi-pro for Old Style Lager and the Plymouth Home Grocers in the '30s and filled in on Dizzy and Daffy Dean's 1934 barn-storming team that would often cross paths with the unhittable Satchel Paige. Gramps loved to cite Dizzy's homespun stories and syntax like: "He slud into third," or "The doc examined my head, but found nuthin'."

In 1974, Jim Murray of the LA Times eulogized Dean:

"Well, we're all ten years older today. Dizzy Dean is dead and 1934 is gone forever. Another part of our youth fled. You look in the mirror and the small boy no longer smiles back at you; just that sad old man. Dizzy died the other

*day at the age of 11 or 12. The little boy in all of us died
with him. But, for one brief shining afternoon in 1934,
he brought joy to that dreary time when we most needed
it. Dizzy Dean... It's impossible to say without a smile, but
then who wants to try? If I know ol' Diz, he'll be calling
God 'podner' someplace today. He might have been what
baseball, is all about."*

'Ol Diz' was the tonic in a game that Americans needed
as a bracer against hopelessness when economics ran dry. The
box score was a daily morality play with good guys in white
pinstripes versus bad guys in the greyness of uncertainty. The
game once carried a flame of hope for Americans that kept
us young. The unofficial slogan, "wait til next year" became
synonymous with optimism and fortitude.

On Dad's side, Grandpa Pickett knew about fortitude. He
lived through a WWI artillery barrage in Europe that tore
up his body and poisoned his eyesight. He returned home to
survive a flu epidemic that killed 50 million people including
675,000 Americans.

One of his simple pleasures was a transistor radio that
carried the voice of the Millers then the Twins: Halsey Hall.
On Sundays, our grandparents often attended noon church
services where Gramps would pull a sleight-of-hand switcheroo
of his hearing aid for a radio earphone, and Halsey would be
preaching the apostles of baseball in a pre-game homily.

Gramps passed in the summer of '79 and the '80s brought a
whole new chapter to my baseball life. I couldn't hit a curveball
but could occasionally turn on a phrase for the Augsburg
College student newspaper. The sports beat implanted me
on the team bus that took us to Reed's Springs, MO, and the

Sho-Me Baseball Camp for spring training in '82. As the bus rolled through Iowa and Missouri to the Ozarks, I taught the guys how to play a card game called "Pitch" that my brother, grandparents, and I played every night at the farm. It's a variation of Euchre that's popular in states where everyone loved Dizzy Dean.

John Turner and I were doing pretty well one evening at a back-hills joint called Bouncing Betty's when Betty subtly informed me the Ozark mountaineers might not appreciate losing money to "carpet-bagging Yankee boys." We didn't need to be showed. We made sure we broke even, made peace with our southern brothers, and headed back to camp.

By 1983, the farm had become my Puff the Magic Dragon — the land was still there, but the baseball people, the radio in the shade of the big maple, and the tractor tube I used for a pitch-back were all gone. But, as a function of humanity, baseball has a way of reinventing itself. Augsburg drew kids from small towns throughout the state, and I was introduced to a marvelous culture that is uniquely Minnesota: Town Team baseball.

Other states have adult amateur baseball, but not like the North Star State where more than 300 teams play ball from the Canadian border to Iowa — in leagues named Land o' Ducks, Lake & Pine, Arrowhead, and Red River. Several college buddies played summer ball for the Willmar Rails in western Minnesota, and I hopped on board for visits to a dozen or more classic small-town venues.

Each town had their own local legends, and all sold cans of beer from an icy five-gallon bucket for a dollar. The flame-thrower, Gary Vien of Montevideo went to "The U", Atwater's speedy Mike Kingery broke in to the Bigs with the Royals, Dana Keicker of Fairfax pitched in the World Series for the Red

Sox, and Jim Eisenreich of St. Cloud batted .361 for the Phillies. I don't recall the name of the forty-seven-year-old hurler for the Raymond Rockets because everyone just called him "Wily Veteran Lefthander."

For those of us prone to nostalgia, baseball is a wonderfully endless escape into 150 years of personalities, stats, and provocative memorabilia from Cooperstown to the Pacific Coast League, the Carolinas, and the Nimrod Gnats of the Lake & Pine.

My favorite piece of paraphernalia from the past was a plastic AM radio at long-gone Culla's Bar in Minneapolis. It had a Grain Belt beer logo, the slogan "been a long time a-brewing" and a line score to be updated in wax pencil as patrons listened to games – presumably to cover for one of my favorite announcers, Herb Carneal, who could go an hour or so without mentioning the score.

When I asked Ma Culla if the radio was spoken for if she ever sold the place, you would have thought I asked for her Scottish grandmother's wedding ring. Ma always had an edge, but she didn't even snort out a sarcastic laugh. Hers was a perfectly dingy beer-and-peanuts joint that was a great place to listen to a Twins game, study, or challenge a handful of profs when *Jeopardy* came on at four o'clock.

At 10:31 pm, on October 25, 1987, Minnesota finally won a cigar. That's the moment the Twins vanquished decades of heartbreaks and redeemed the soul of our favorite son in the stadium we named for him, the Hubert Horatio Humphrey Metrodome. The place was slightly better than the worst ballpark in history – Tropicana Field in Tampa – and from the outside "The Dome" looked like one of America's Roadside Attractions: the world's largest tin of Jiffy Pop Popcorn.

But it was our popcorn stand, and in the spirit of Mr. Humphrey, the state boldly declared "We Like it Here" in large block letters beyond the right field line. The championship was bittersweet for me as it came at the expense of my grandmother and the Cardinals. But they already had nine titles, so I got over it by 10:32.

The '90s were a new chapter altogether again – except the decade started with another World Championship. By this time, I was implementing marketing programs in the world of sports, and all dialed in with behind-the-scenes access to the bowels of stadiums where major league baseball made its sausage. The access came from my bosses who had worked in the sausage factory, then figured out how to escape the grind by leveraging the personalities, stats, and memorabilia in consumer promotions for major brands like Wheaties and Snickers; gone were the fifteen-hour days and constant pressure to win and sell, then sell and win.

A former Twins executive turned co-worker, and one of the most pragmatic and unselfish men I've ever met, Mark Weber, is a Minnesota baseball legend to the little people. He'd skim booty from Candyland in the locker room, or from piles of promotional items, then share like Robin Hood with ticket takers, custodians, and parking lot attendants. He recognized my love of the game and advised me to not get too close. Because of him, I didn't have to, but got plenty of plunder anyway. Trying to repay favors to "Web" was like trying to hit Satchel Paige, you could fantasize about it, but it could only happen with pure luck.

My baseball luck arrived in circumstance and coincidence for more than a decade. The St. Paul Saints minor league club was reborn on my 32nd birthday and threw a big party. A few buddies and I had flight benefits that took us on day trips to Wrigley, Fenway, Busch, and Tiger Stadium. I had a client who was a key supplier to the Red Sox and we watched a game from *inside* the Green Monster. One September, the boys and I were scheduled to fly to Milwaukee to watch Gram's Cardinals play. The day before we left, four planes went down, then every ballgame and every flight in the hemisphere was cancelled for weeks.

As a designer of promotional marketing programs, I travelled around the country to sports venues and would occasionally find myself in a seat next to a personality who brought statistics to life. I worked for several weeks at a time at the Phoenix Open golf tournament in Scottsdale and often dined bar side at Don & Charlie's steak house. Baseball's spring training was ramping up at the same time, and an old timer who saddled up next to me asked, "What's your story, kid? Where you from?"

"St. Paul," I replied.

"St. Paul, not Minneapolis," he said with a knowing nod. "I know St. Paul. I struck out 20 of you bastards for Louisville in '49."

It was Mickey McDermott, who ended up with those Yankees. I noticed his World Series ring had a '56' on it and asked, gape-mouthed, where he was when Don Larsen threw the only perfect game in World Series history.

"In the bullpen eatin' Phil Rizutto's spaghetti!" he said as if he still had one over on "Scooter" fifty years later.

McDermott didn't have a lick of humility, but he sure had the gift of gab, and I enjoyed it for a couple hours that night.

Back in St. Paul, where he set the minor league strike-out record, my wife and I got to meet the antithesis to his personality, at – of all places – a St. Paul Saints game.

The unpretentious Buck O'Neil was better in person than he was in Ken Burns' film, *Baseball*, that documented his patience and forgiveness for languishing in the Negro Leagues when he had the talent to be playing in the majors.

You couldn't just meet and greet Mr. O'Neil. He was too engaging. Before you knew it, he was telling stories about his departed wife, Ora Lee, flashing his infectious smile, and graciously talking about his good fortune.

True baseball people are that way, they approach every at-bat with optimism, and hopefully "wait til next year" in the off season.

True baseball people, however, aren't seen at every East Coast streetcar station or in the Midwest cornfields as they once were. A tattered, "Win Twins" Louisville Slugger with a nail through its heart has been replaced with modern composites and hearts of aluminum.

The game has been squeezed like polymers into American pockets while hungry kids in Dominican neighborhoods are hitting anything shaped like a ball with anything shaped like a stick.

Voices grow dim then slip off to where ever that big ol' maple with a radio is now casting its shade; but I'll keep listening with the spirit of my grandfather for new voices to emerge – as did baseball 100 years ago… when World War I, the Spanish Flu and the Black Sox scandal tried to kill it; after the greed of a strike stole the summer of '94, and more recently in the new millennium when Industrial Age memories were tainted by performance enhancing needles that point to artists who became artificial.

Our "wait til next year" was a bit longer in 2020 as the fearful uncertainty of another pandemic measured our fortitude and postponed all kinds of "Opening Days."

It wasn't the first nasty slider we'd ever seen… it was déjà vu all over again.

When our national pastimes returned, the rules were different, and a lot of folks were too scared to come out of the dugout; but the true baseball people took a deep breath, dug in, then faced the next at-bat with a fresh count and the renewed optimism of a brand-new season.

PART THIRTY-TWO

ROYAL OVERSIGHT

I should have listened to my wife. She's usually right.

I don't mean that in the acquiescent, emasculated sort of way, the one that is so *en vogue* these days. In the first place, she'd never expect, or accept that tone. It's simply a data-driven fact that my wife is more perceptive than I on such matters. She's more pragmatic, less prone to be swayed by idealism or nostalgia, she doesn't bear the yoke of needing to be right all the time, and – remarkably – she only says 'I told you so' with her eyes.

When I shook off her suggestion as if she were trying to pitch me on a *People Magazine* subscription, she said only, "Arright."

But I should have listened. Upon reflection, the situation was much like when I once departed to perform the duties of public address announcing at an outdoor soccer, or futball game, as it were. I'm a well-seasoned veteran of open-air, autumnal activities in Minnesota. I've lived most of my life in the USDA's "purple" plant-hardiness zone. And yet, for some inexplicable reason, I under-dressed for the occasion and was uncomfortable throughout.

Similarly, when a woman who has for more than three decades, had only my best interest at heart – makes a suggestion

– one would think I would give it more credence than that of an encouragement to devolve into mindless consumption of tabloid journalism.

So, I should have listened when she said, "You'd like *The Crown.*"

My wife had been watching the popular Netflix series on "date-nights" with a gal-pal for a couple of years, for a while, it was in pandemic style, with synced cell phones while they consumed wine and bags of cheez-puffs in virtual connectivity.

But, as I said, I neglected the counsel. I looked at her with a moderately incredulous notion that she must be slipping. How on earth could she believe I would have any interest whatsoever in the fashions and foibles of Royal life?

As pandemic orders lingered, Mary Beth and I got a bit better at choosing mutually enjoyable movies from 14,526 selections, but it was obvious my wife preferred the virtual gal-night binge consumption with her friend. She'd retreat to her reading and binge-watching chair, I to the den. They'd take in *Ray Donovan*, or *House of Cards*, as I pecked on the computer and re-watched *Perry Mason*, or *Andy Griffith*.

I finally broke down one evening after rewinding, and mouthing along with "It's me, it's me, it's Ernest T!" during a Mayberry classic.

Earlier in the evening, my wife had made one last, desperate plea for me to watch *The Crown*.

"I wouldn't have pegged John Lithgow as Churchill," she said in passing. "He was great."

Churchill? I thought. Is it possible this isn't a sappy, TV serial version of an Emma Thompson, Kenneth Branagh, or Kate Winslet movie? Might there be some historical context to the drivel? As Perry Mason broke an unwitting suspect on the stand, and Opie said, "It's OK, Pa," I reluctantly, and hopefully said to the remote: "The Crown."

It's too soon to say where the supercilious Royals will rank in comparison to the other three series I've binged, but they're locked in a stretch drive with *Band of Brothers*, *Mad Men*, and *The Sopranos*. After I'd watched Season One, my wife cautioned about falling for lead actress, Claire Foy. I told her, "Too late," I'm a wanna-be Don Draper, working an angle to make her my girlfriend.

That binge-watching stuff can get in one's head. That's why I can't go to the content and imagery of *Breaking Bad*, *Walking Dead*, or the darkness of current-day genres. I have to fast-forward through uncomfortable, historically resolved scenarios from 80 years ago.

I don't know about you but, for me, a six-episode binge evening invariably leads to an altered dream state. I closed the Lucky Strike account and wooed an un-wooable woman as a Mad man. I single-handedly liberated a town in Belgium on behalf of my brothers, and Tony Soprano trusted me as his calming consigliere.

TV-time in the more genteel land of the United Kingdom led to different emotions and reflection. I was impressed with much of the historical accuracy and realism of *The Crown's* early seasons; so much so that, as I divined the accuracy with constant Google searches, my online ad feeds became flooded with Royal reference to the very tabloidish information I wished to avoid.

The sets, wardrobes, and acting was so comprehensive – down to the mannerisms. I was reminded of what a significant and positive world-figure Queen Elizabeth II had been, of her singular sense of duty and resilience, and that I'd rather live with a bloodhound in a hillbilly shack than with royal blood in a tower of London.

As we all know, the mind works in mysterious ways, and – in dream – takes us down fascinating, sometimes ridiculous paths. I very much enjoyed the book, *Remains of the Day* by Kazuo Ishiguro, and the accompanying movie starring Dame Emma Thompson (who's two days older than my wife) and Sir Anthony Hopkins.

The movie version of Ishiguro's novel – about an English butler and his unstated love of a housekeeper – collided with a Netflix docudrama in a dream one night as I found myself in a UK pub after running out of gas on a stone-walled road. I sat reserved and respectful, in the British spirit, until the locals finally embraced my Yankeeness with an inquisition.

"I say, you're American?" The Welsh, or Liverpudlian, or South African, or Australian accent politely asked.

"I am," I replied, with as much mutual respect as a revolutionary could imply.

"What then, if I may ask, does one think of our monarchical system of government?"

I paused in deference to company, then replied, "I have oft' pondered the subject, and with your permission, sir, would offer an extended riposte."

"Please do, sir," was the response, in a regal – not Liverpudlian, Welsh, and certainly not Scottish – accent.

"As a Yank, I am partial to republicanism, but must admit, my fellow colonists have little knowledge of the concept. They insist the United States is a democracy, and rather behave as unwitting dolts at election time. Depending upon the fate of their chosen parties, they ascend to tyranny, or digress to common mobs of anarchy."

I paused to sip of ice-chilled Beefeater – I must have been in England.

"Please continue, sir."

"Well," I honored his request, "my co-patriots are primarily an ignorant lot who would presume the Magna Carta to be a large menu. They are wholly unaware of the necessity for representative government to protect the individual's rights above the state, and that, had our founders not contrived such a condition, the entire world would today be lorded over by tyrannical despots."

I swirled my glass, but not wishing to appear indulgent, set it back down. "I, myself, am a Free-Will man who endorses the inalienable rights of the Creator. So long as we're all equal under the law, I find no fear in another who has, or claims to possess, a divine place in government. Many American bureaucrats do so."

The man shifted in his chair, obviously shocked that a Yank had an opinion beyond commercial appeal. A few others snuck closer in curiosity.

"I say," he said in whatever accent, "You are most imparted with specific opinion. And what of our monarchy?"

I stroked my chin, then did sip of the juniper. "Far be it from me to presume," I implored. "As stated,

I am a devout republican – not of party, but of archetype – but I see great value in the fluid transformation of your constitutional monarchy."

Some leaned in, some leaned out. Perhaps the dream-place was Wales.

"I admit to a limited understanding of your constitutional process, but as an admitted capitalist Yank, I stand in envy."

The Loyalists and anti-royals went quizzical alike.

"I find myself curious, sir," the inquisitor inquired. "How so?"

"The math is quite simple," I replied. "I know of no colonist who wouldn't leap at the chance to pay our "head of state" the equivalent of 100 million pounds, tender that mouth to suggestive irrelevance, then reap two billion pounds from perpetually envious tourists who gape at the caged exhibition. My dear friends," I continued, "Your Buckingham Palace is a nationalized version of our Disneyland."

Strains of *Rule Britannia* filled the air as the crowd nodded and proudly toasted one and other to the clever evolution of their realm.

I awoke and returned from Swansea, or Nottingham, to the sound of my wife's voice. "You were up late," she said. "It's good, isn't it?"

A groggy sense of sorrowful compassion for the Royals and their divine entrapments blended with Don Draper's self-imposed misery. Tony Soprano's immature violence met the selfless sacrifice of the 101st Airborne.

"It's terrific," I said as my head cleared, then repeated an axiom we both embraced, "... but... everything you need to know, you can learn from *The Andy Griffith Show*."

PART THIRTY-THREE

YESTERDAY AND TOMORROW

My brother, Ringo, has Pop's library of classic, and musty old books. He inherited them after none of us kids had the guts to throw them away. Facing St. Peter is one thing, but the prospect of having mom greet you at the pearly gates with, "your father wants to speak to you," kind of dampened the whole heaven thing, so the books are still in the family.

Ringo was on epidemic leave and hunkered down to open *John Adams*, by Charles Page Smith. The inherited relic still had stains from the house fire in '71, along with a provenance inside the front cover – a hand-written note from mom. Ringo shot me a text photo, and we shared an emotional moment before he even got to the forward.

Mom read and signed the book in '63; she left us in '76, a bicentennial after Adams signed the Declaration and 150 years after his death. He and his dear friend and co-signer, Thomas Jefferson, both died on July 4, 1826; the 50th Anniversary of the liberating document, in an historic reminder of the difference between coincidence – running into a friend at Home Depot – and a divine moment.

People used to write their names inside the covers of books – to stake a claim or leave a tiny breadcrumb to mark a step in one's journey. John and Abigail Adams left more crumbs than most of us, but we each have a journey to nurture – a trail to blaze on the route to the manifestation of our beliefs.

"From yesterday we get the blueprints of tomorrow!!" mom wrote in impeccable script; the underlines of 'yesterday' and 'tomorrow', with two exclamation points at the end was her version of a Five Star revue as well as a 'note to self' and whomever may find her breadcrumb.

She was 31 years old in '63 and had six kids – with another on the way – but she somehow found time to read the book about the nation's desperate struggle to change the way humans envisioned and realized their role on this planet. Our mom, like an Adams, was one of those people who could put 110 pounds of nails in a 100 lb. keg and carry it on the hip that wasn't holding a kid.

John and Abigail would have liked us as neighbors when the Revolution was brewing like a tea bag in Boston Harbor. We're more like the Addams Family on the television sitcom than the founding family, but Dad was the Commanding Officer of the Marine Detachment on the aircraft carrier, USS Bennington – and mom was like a Sargent-Major. They were patriots in the truest sense of the word and the types who would "pledge their lives, fortunes, and sacred honor" for the sake of others.

In one of her rebellious moments, mom challenged the status quo – and the values of her chosen political party – at a public hearing to discuss sex education within Burnsville's Independent School District #191. Our parents were Republicans back when the GOP was conservative, and cared. It was 1972, years prior to the union's vote to oust parents from "Education-Minnesota" and declare a collective bargaining cartel worthy of the King's Acts of Sedition.

Once upon a time, school districts were guided by a collaboration between the PTA (Parent Teacher Association), along with teachers unions, and locally elected school boards. Union annexation began in the late 70s; formal capitulation by parent-citizens occurred in 1998, without so much as a spilled cup of tea.

The public forum in Burnsville was convened to discuss whether the reproduction process should be taught in classrooms or exclusively at home. This was long before one's emotional disposition could supersede the biological character of their genetic chromosomes, and at a time when access to pornography was generally limited to semi-nude pictures in Playboy Magazines stolen from dumpsters - or twenty-five-cent biology lessons at skid row Peep Shows.

Mom was running for School Board, got hold of the mic, energized a minority, and eliminated her chance at election. It was counter-intuitive – certainly counter-political – for a conservative to take a position against the sanctity of such an intimate parental responsibility, but she did it. She challenged the attendees as to whether they knew how to properly educate their children on the issue, and if they even had the nerve to do so. Her challenge was very succinct:

"You want 'em to learn it in the back seat of a Chevy like our generation did?" she belted into the mic.

The room exploded in a combination of laughter, gasps, cheers, and catcalls. Mom continued on her soap box as the chair pounded the gavel and finally declared, "Mrs. Pickett, if you want to run for school board, rent your own hall!"

A few seconds later, people started throwing coins at the stage. The chair instructed the ushers to "Get her out of here!" but it took a while as she was surrounded by sister Chell's friends on the football team – who were state champions, by the way. The jocks threw coins and formed a huddle around mom as poor Chell slumped in her metal folding chair. Mom didn't win the election, but reproduction was added to the health curriculum.

As she was reading the book rediscovered by Ringo, Mom must have been inspired when she came across reference to James Otis Jr.

John Adams said Otis had a "reckless vitality." Otis coined the phrase "taxation without representation is tyranny." He renounced his position as Advocate General of the Admiralty Court (Attorney General in today's terms) to argue against the British Parliament and the King for their oppressive "Writs of Assistance," along with the Townshend, Stamp, Sugar, Molasses, and Acts of Sedition that were smothering colonists with the "deliberate intellectual confusion" of legal and financial mandates.

Otises' definition of liberty was simple and authentic: "The colonists are by the law of nature freeborn - as indeed all men are - white or black."

Otis is attributed with galvanizing the voices of liberty in a five-hour argument against the writs in 1761. He influenced and colluded with Adams, Jefferson, Franklin, and Thomas Paine for a decade before sporadic mental illness, then a blow to the head from a British tax collector left him as a recluse. He is regarded by historians to be one of the most influential – and forgotten – heroes of the Revolution.

The signature of Patty Ann Pickett, would have looked great at the bottom of the Declaration of Independence next to James Otis Jr.

The signatures of the "Recklessly vital" are written instead in a special realm; one populated by the souls of the overlooked and little known – people who fight for human rights as a natural condition of their spirits, and the belief that no other spirit – regardless of race, creed, or emotional gender disposition – deserves less than mutual love, respect, and equality under the law.

That realm is the most crowded place in heaven, and the loneliest on earth.

PART THIRTY-FOUR

FOR THE LOVE OF PETE

It had been fourteen weeks, ninety-eight days, since the First Law of Thermal Dynamics became the only thing that mattered to our dear friend, Peter Stathopoulos. The First Law insists that "energy is neither created nor destroyed." Pete was within moments of passing and had to transform his courage into whatever shape a spirit takes when it leaves its mortal form.

Heisenberg's uncertainty principle: "there is inherent uncertainty in the act of measuring a variable," led to proof that human thought has actual mass. According to scientists, "a lifetime of average thought has the weight of a mosquito."

For Pete, it must have been a June bug.

Lou Gehrig's disease, Amyotrophic Lateral Sclerosis… ALS… enforced the law and the transformation of Pete on April 10th of 2021.

The celebration of his former self took place on July 17th in his parents' back yard; a spacious suburban plot with a swimming pool and a gate that opens to the neighborhood park where Pete and his grade school cronies logged infinite hours of energy creation as they played hockey, baseball, and "The Ghost is Out Tonight."

His family and a cadre of loving friends invested hours of Zoom calls and physical excuses to gather, for Pete's sake, to plan the event. Tents for shade, food from his favorite restaurant, mood and celebratory music by a compassionate brother-sister act who performed as if their hearts weren't breaking on every note.

One of the cadre is a good Joe - another courageous spirit. Our Joe has the delicate skill to guide a touchy, 500-pound wheelchair for an incapacitated friend, and a patient willingness to drive a custom mini-van loaded with repressed energy. Joe would open and close the remembrances that day. He introduced neighbor Jim for a couple of great kid stories and an opening prayer before handing the mic to me.

My role was to talk about the writer. It was Pete's most prominent passion, and one we shared.

I had ninety-eight days to write the words and treated it a lot like a freshman comp assignment. Mary Beth heard me babbling the night before at 9 p.m., then that very day at two and five a.m. She sensed I wasn't comfortable with the delivery.

"You want to read it to me?" she asked.

I paused in personal absorption, then acquiesced. She had guided me through Pop's, and her father's eulogies, so I agreed. A generous wordsmith had helped me through last-minute editing, but Pete, my usual voice critic, wasn't available. Who else could I trust?

"You're reading," she said. "Stop it. You need to express."

"The words are nice," she added in a tone that was critique in neither way.

I looked at my wife and saw my grandmother in a cotton dress and floured apron giving me unemotional direction.

I didn't know if she knew how hard this one was, if she realized how much Pete meant to me. She may have sensed that I was obsessed with what people would think of my words, and how I would sound, rather than the responsibility of honoring our friend.

"I know," I said. But didn't.

An hour before the presentations, I broke away from the party to a pantry cove in the basement of the Stathopoulos home to read and re-read til I got it right; but it never happened. I kept reading, and stammering instead, and thinking about omitting adjectives on the fly to trick the reading into sounding like expression. I gave up, then said four and a half of five Memorare prayers to Mary, begging for a miraculous intercession.

A hockey-playing nephew of Pete's wandered down to look for an open bathroom – or a utility tub to pee in – and stole the last half of the fifth prayer.

Four must have been good enough; Mary swiped back the momentum and hit me with a beautiful pass. After Jim's opening prayer, I took a deep breath, and began to express...

Edward Everett was the featured speaker at the consecration of Gettysburg Cemetery. Abe Lincoln was invited as a formal courtesy. There were no Netflix binge-series back then, and Everett was a brilliant speaker who would rent himself out to perform historic lectures that were two or three hours long.

Lincoln delivered his Gettysburg Address after the Everett docudrama, and the headliner responded to the president about the "eloquent simplicity & appropriateness" of his remarks. In the note, Everett said, "I should be glad, if

I could flatter myself that I came as near to the central idea of the occasion in two hours, as you did in two minutes."

There you all sit, hoping we can give you Peter Stathopoulos in a Lincoln moment. That's not going to happen. But we will give you some thoughts to ponder, and in less than half an hour.

As complex as Pete was, his beauty was in eloquent simplicity. He got brains and sweetness from his mother, and the depth of ancient Greece from his father. Peter is an old soul that reflects the truths of his favorite philosopher, Socrates, who is credited with saying, "Be kind, for everyone you meet is fighting a difficult battle."

Pete lived the Ten Commandments… as if they were an obvious office memo about not eating your co-worker's peanut butter and jelly sandwiches. He honored parables as most of us do traffic signs. He was tolerant and forgiving, yet unwavering… like a modern-day Gandhi. He loved with absolute sincerity.

The ancient gods gave Pete a dutiful spirit, and he became Sisyphus, pushing a rock of hope up a hill every day for his kids, family, friends, and caregivers.

We saw the rock at the bottom of the hill each day and did our best to join the futile effort. Our childhood cronies rallied around Pete and his family here at Bev and Jim's, and the family, like dogs who are said to be rescued, rescued us back with unconditional love.

We all were fired up when Pete told us about a new doctor, a compassionate pioneer in ALS treatment named Merit Cudkowicz; she's the Chief of Neurology and Director of the ALS Clinic at Massachusetts General Hospital, as well as a professor of neurology at Harvard.

I said to him, "Oh my, Pete, how great is it to work with her?" He blinked a few times and said, "She's amazing. You wouldn't believe the access she gives me." Then he added, in true Yale fashion, "I do have to dumb down my language, of course."

Pete loved Yale. He respected the traditions but talked mostly about the cast of characters... his pal with the naughty nickname... the one that got away... a Dean that let him skip off to Europe, and selfless friends who pledged endless resources to purchase one ray of hope... or a day off, for Sisyphus Pete. His stories of the people of Yale made me wish I had studied more in high school.

When physical Pete departed, he left many of us alone on desert islands of thoughts that you would share only with Peter Stathopoulos. He could talk about anything; the parallels of ancient Greece to modern culture, the writings of Virginia Woolf or Dylan Thomas, the music of Bob Dylan, Mozart, or Led Zeppelin. He lived his life above the fracas of partisan politics and is the most universal person most of us will ever meet. He's missed on a level that is impossible to comprehend... I guess, partly, because none of us has ever lost a romantic, stoic, metaphysical smart-ass before.

One thing Pete wouldn't talk about – is work. Only the people… their personalities and perspectives, and how they influenced his life. The work was just a means to an end… to feed and educate his children and set himself up for early retirement so he could wake, write, take a long walk, then write some more.

The closest Peter ever came to expressing frustration to me was when he mentioned he had come within months of realizing that long-time dream. We watched him forgive God and thankfully dig into a mandated early retirement with voice-activated software.

Peter's prose was enchanting… but he admittedly struggled with closing paragraphs. It's as if he didn't want to finish… didn't want to leave. None of us wanted Pete to leave, and we lived for many months in denial that it would ever happen. It did, of course. Even the immortal among us meet transformation.

Pete and I shared a love of writing and declared that we were muses to each other. He is my greatest source of inspiration, but historically, a muse is an alluring goddess. I asked him how I ended up with the ugliest muse on the planet.

But he's my muse… my personal Pete. The Gods made him especially for me. You all know he's mine… because he's yours in the same way. His spirit is ubiquitous, like the Grand Canyon, the Mississippi River, or the Acropolis.

Virginia Woolf wrote, "For if it is rash to walk into a lion's den unarmed, rash to navigate the Atlantic in a rowing boat, rash to stand on one foot atop of St. Paul's, it is still more rash to go home alone with a poet."

And yet, we all did. We went home with the poet, Peter Stathopoulos, with the philosopher, the hockey player, the street musician, the classmate. We went with the deck-mate on an ocean freighter, the marketing executive, the father, the sibling, the son. We went with a trust that was never violated, and we came away with a heart more kind, and the enduring impression of an ancient spirit.

Thank you, Peter, and God Bless you.

The delivery probably wasn't great, but it was sincere, and there was almost no way to disappoint the loving and forgiving crowd. The expression, in the name of Pete, was achieved. There were glints of appreciation, in tears, from at least a few.

I had no tears that day. I took deep breaths, and my wife for granted, as I continued in my self-absorbed honoring of a selfless person. I'm overly sentimental to begin with, and had been pre-suppressing my emotions, for my sake, for a week.

Joe wrapped up the formality with grace, then opened the mic to the crowd. Our friend Karen is an airline captain who had come directly to the event after 22 hours of travel. She had been in Pete's beloved Greece the day before and climbed to the Acropolis to get closer to him and say a prayer.

There was a fascinating college friend named Eric. He and Pete shared a Harvard-Yale rivalry, then tin cups in France as they strummed instruments for passersby. They parted and agreed to meet one year later at the Eiffel tower, but it was An Affair to Not Remember, and there were no cell phones. After reuniting in the States, they hit the road again and camped one night under a bridge, and debated whether it was more wise to run or fight together if bandits appeared.

"I'm not running," Eric said.

"Run or fight?" became their personal catchphrase.

I hugged and talked with Pete's mom and had a long-awaited cocktail with his dad. Mary Beth was ready to leave – it had been five hours, and her cousin was playing in a band at a brew pub beer garden - but she let me finish my drink and conversation.

On the drive to the beer garden, she sensed my need for decompression and said, "we can just go home if you'd like."

I did want to go home, but sensed I owed her.

The name of the band was "Tangled up in Dylan," a coincidental… perhaps pre-destined tribute to Pete's favorite balladeer, the guy he imitated on street corners in Paris, Berlin, and New York City.

The band began to play *The Times They Are A-Changin'…* for the love of Pete… I wept in the middle of a crowded beer garden.

PART THIRTY-FIVE

FLIGHT 131

A flight from Chicago O'Hare to Minneapolis/St. Paul takes less than an hour. There have been more than a million flights between the cities in my lifetime and I've done it at least a hundred times. One in the hundred, one in a million, was with my sister, and it changed the way I look at life.

As Amelia Earhart once said, "There's more to life than being a passenger."

I used to fly a lot for business – a millennium ago – and was rewarded with the loyalty incentives of the day. In addition to seat upgrades, drink coupons, and free headsets that plugged in to a miniature version of Spotify – I had employee benefits on Northwest Airlines thanks to my wife, Mary Beth, who was a consummate sales pro for the MSP-based fleet of aircraft.

In 1989, two years after she was hired, the airline was purchased by corporate investors who began the process of "upgrading the brand," a.k.a., "fatting the calf." The brand-conscious bean-counters turned 63 years of accumulated assets into liquid loyalty incentives to be sipped away by senior executives.

As an employee of the airline robber-barons, my wife received two-thirds salary, one-third flights to dream destinations that cost us – and the corporate raiders – nothing. Who was I to complain about leveraged buyouts? The trickle-down perks allowed me to fly to Chicago, meet with a client in Oak Park, have lunch at The Berghoff, fly home, and replace the flapper on a leaky toilet... all before my buddy, Mark Weber, who consulted for an industrial manufacturer could even get to Fargo, North Dakota.

One day, the perkful access to Chicago lifted me beyond corporate aspiration and allowed me to fly with the oldest of my five sisters on the day her doctors would issue a prognosis on a malignant growth.

Chell and I boarded Flight 131 at O'Hare for the short hop to MSP. The taxi from the gate to take-off was longer than the flight, so cabin attendants hurried to make positive brand impressions on behalf of the new-age robber-barons with rapid distribution of cocktails and Spanish peanuts.

We were over Rockford then southern Wisconsin within moments as we chatted about the miserable condition of Chicago streets and the perpetual corruption of Cook County politics, but Chell had some news to share, and I knew she wasn't going to chit-chat all the way to Menomonie.

"It's 99-to-one," she said, with matter-of-fact resolve.

Chell and three of my five sisters had brushes with threatening cysts and lumps. The Cancer showed up in my little sister, Missy, and she mocked it in an Uncle Fester costume then laughed at it til it slinked away. The sister who hasn't had a threat is just flat-out meaner than disease. Cancer, like a lone hyena, stalks that lioness, too, but she just glares back to let the jackal know who'd be the dish du jour if he tried anything.

My sisters are all like that – nasty tough when challenged. They're fierce and loving, controlling, imperfect and manic, each in her own special way. My female ancestors and cousins were and are that way, too. I see the characteristics in nieces and daughter as well, and I guess I instinctively married into the traits.

My oldest sister though, became the empress of tough in our family and a composite of Queen Victoria, Cleopatra, Rosa Parks, Joan of Arc, and Mother Teresa – whom she once encountered at an airport in India:

"I was pecking at my laptop when a murmur came flowing down the concourse. I couldn't help but look up to see a tiny woman in a white habit with powder-blue stripes. She strolled without emotion down the center of the walkway as crowds of people parted like the Red Sea. Here was this Catholic nun in a nation of Hindus, Buddhists, Sikhs, and Muslims… and every person paused and bowed with respect. It's the most powerful moment I've ever experienced."

My sister became an influential person – not because she craved power, or the inherent grace of Mother Teresa. My sister, like the world's Sister of Calcutta, interpreted her gifts as a responsibility.

Chell started earning her Tech stripes in the early dawn of the Age by correcting her high school math teacher in 1969 as he taught 'Basic BASIC' computer classes. She wasn't insubordinate, she was incapable of accepting an inaccurate mathematical equation.

As she might say, *"Hello…? That would defeat the whole purpose of mathematics."*

In her role as a woman who was early to the rank of tech exec – in a time that preceded the WorldWideWeb in The

Cloud – math met politics for my sister in boardrooms that had been boys-only not long before. Chell knew when to act like she didn't care when the boys excluded her from rounds of golf (even without knowing she'd probably win). She learned her patient tactics from our Pop, a Naval Academy Marine, who taught her to wait for the right moment to react. Pop advised her to step carefully and avoid the self-destructive snare of the trap. Her favorite line from the 'Lectures of Rex' was: "There is no failure, only delayed success."

When the boys excluded her, Chell cared, but intuitively knew they were dinosaurs, and how the future would be redemptive. She didn't compete with a gender; some men were brilliant mentors and collaborators… some, boorish pigs. She – and her female contemporaries – were leveraging their will against an archaic caste system with hopes of nudging the human inequity of this world toward the perfect balance of the universe.

As the oldest of seven kids, Chell was automatically on a pedestal, but she earned every step. She was kind as a babysitter even when our neediness frayed her nerves. She was a Hula Hoop champ as a teen in the '60s even with a dislocated elbow from a gymnastics mishap. The straight-A student was runner-up as Junior Miss Queen and salutatorian at Burnsville High School in 1972.

The second-place finishes affirmed the Lectures of Rex.

Her first adult brush with the boorish pig side of maleness came as a model for a television commercial. After one day on a set in Green Bay, she knew it was best to not separate the words 'pretty' and 'smart.'

Chell would come to wear accumulated wisdom in an aura or – as her sisters might say – as a tiara. She laughed with the rest of us when, just after she had been featured on the cover of a Tech Magazine, another sister said, "Back off, Miss High-and-Mighty. We all knew you when you ate sliced hot dogs and Velveeta cheese over pork and beans – and liked it."

It was appropriate that Chell and I were flying from her home state of Illinois. Before I knew it as the 'Land of Lincoln' I knew the spirits, willpower, and DNA of our Illinois mother, grandmother, and aunts Edith, Alice, Helen, and Lena; women who passed their no-nonsense personas and essential toughness on to following generations.

Chell and I were just south of Mt. Hope, Wisconsin on Flight 131 when she shared the 99-to-one prognosis.

"Huh?" I replied.

"The prognosis. It's 99-to-one… against," she repeated.

My face went blank with an unbelieving stare.

Chell had been my substitute mom since '76. I lived with her and former husband Russ my senior year of high school after mom died and Pop moved to the western suburbs. Chell and Russ loaned me money when they shouldn't have, let me drive their cool cars, and took me to Vikings' games back when Minnesota was the only place in the country that had tailgating. They supplemented my flannel shirt wardrobe with elegant sweaters and shoes that were worthy of polish. Chell demonstrated a path to a better, more comfortable life at the most crucial time for an impressionable young mind.

She gave me the inside information that women would look at my fingernails and footwear for first impressions.

On Flight 131, my sister watched as I reverted from a cocky, emerging businessman with a Platinum WorldPerks card, to a sullen child who was flashing back to 1965 when she cuddled him and two younger sisters in a Bloomington basement as tornadoes were ravaging the region and mom and dad were off with a suburban planning committee.

On Flight 131, the matriarch who I trusted implicitly, watched me wonder if I could endure the loss of two moms in two decades. The condemned woman lifted herself beyond the condition with consoling eyes as mine began to glisten. But I was supposed to be there to support her, and I flattened my lips in my best imitation of her mentor – our father. It was, perhaps, my first-ever attempt at acting like a grownup.

A cabin attendant arrived with perfect timing to offer another round of grownup beverages to boost my thin bravado. Even though I was completely obsessed with my own emotion, I found a way to ask about hers.

"What's going through your mind, Chell?" I asked. "How do you feel… mentally?"

In case I haven't encapsulated the level of my sister's pragmatism, she dutifully strolled through the conversation like Teresa down a concourse.

"You know," she said, "at first I thought 'why me?' and was really sad. Then I thought, 'why NOT me?'"

My heart sank and was lifted by her grace. She continued.

"I've done well financially and can take care of Dad… and my kids… I can leave fulfilled…' How many people get to take a better bow at the end of the story?"

Chell processed tragic victim status into magnanimous poise in less than two hours between Northwestern Medical Center and O'Hare International. Her perspective inspired, in me, reflections of those women who inspired her and gave her that marvelous DNA. I was processing the probable loss of another of my most beloved women – the one to whom I was closest.

Flight 131 made an ominous landing.

Chell didn't like to lose; she didn't care much for delayed success either, but she tolerated it – and that paid off when she rallied to beat the 99-to-one front-runner in a knock-down, drag-out battle that lasted for months and concluded with her convalescing in a converted family room in my and Mary Beth's St. Paul home. Our meaner-than-disease, lioness sister – who's a nurse – would stop by and sit in a corner doing cross-stitch without saying a word to Chell… she'd just stitch… and keep an eye out for that Jackal.

Chell went on to beat even longer odds when she was named CEO of Cap-Gemini Ernst & Young N.A., a major technology consulting firm… but Cancer wasn't done. A few years later, it returned with a 50-50 prognosis. Chell summoned the willpower of her DNA, pushed the odds to 51-49, then went 2-0 against the disease. Evil promoters of the scourge somehow scheduled a third challenge to my sister, but Vegas odds-makers shook their heads at The Cancer and declared the bet "off the board."

Back-to-back-to-back ass-whoopings of the world's most notorious villain did not, however, come without a price. The bouts and treatments ravaged the insides of my courageous sister, but not her spirit or will. They didn't keep her from a dinner with Bill Gates, a trip to the South Pole, diving in the Indian Ocean, or exploring the Serengeti. She was raised and inspired by tough country women and a little sister of Calcutta – none of whom competed on the basis of gender, race, or creed – but with the power of their will.

Our sister flew millions of miles in her lifetime. I, somehow, got to share a few of the most precious. In 2022 she needed a new kidney, and it was no surprise when her siblings, nieces and nephews lined up to see if they were potential donors, and secretly hoped to give a piece of their flesh to honor our queen.

But none of us were worthy.

Before we could find a match for that marvelous DNA, on July 18th Ann Rochelle departed on a new and endless flight of her very own.

A Tim McGraw song comes to mind. It encourages us to be more aware of our mortality and to consciously live a more fulfilled life. It suggests we all could, *"Love deeper, speak sweeter, give the forgiveness we've been denying, and live like we were dying."*

Our oldest sister did just that... for more than 60 years.

PART THIRTY-SIX

ONE BRIDGE

One of my favorite podcasts is "The Great Stories" – classic narratives of iconic authors produced half-a-world away by Trev Downey, a professor of English in Dublin. He's sometimes joined by a literary pal, Neil Poole, who calls in from the UK. Their analysis is fantastic, but even better is that listening feels like running into them at a neighborhood pub right after you've read what they're reading.

My eyebrows pinched in curiosity as I listened across the pond while they discussed Kate Chopin's *The Story of an Hour*, a short story about the thoughts of a woman after she is told her husband has died in an accident. Downey and Poole always offer insights into the author's life and talked that day of how Kate's father had perished in an 1855 train wreck in central Missouri.

Less than half a day earlier, I'd been doing research for a story of my own, one that I thought had nothing to do with Kate Chopin, an author of whom – I'm embarrassed to say – I knew nothing. In the process, I learned my great-great grandfather, Douglas Aleshire, had survived an 1855 train wreck in central Missouri.

Kate Chopin – born Katherine O'Flaherty – is far too little-known. Like Virginia Woolf, she's a super-powerful storyteller who, more than a century ago, courageously preceded modern feminism with observations of mutual gender truths and real-life inequities. She lost her father at age five, two brothers by the age of 25, and her husband at 32. She didn't give up on men, she just stopped expecting them to be around. At the turn of the 20th Century, she was a champion of individual identity and her writing "broke new ground" before disappearing from the American Literary landscape until the 1970s.

How many 1855 train wrecks could there have been in central Missouri? I wondered as I turned to Google. Sure enough, Kate and I both had family on that train. Knowing my own life and learning of hers brought about parallels. We shared the geography of the central Mississippi River basin, the premature loss of a parent, childhoods dominated by strong women, lost family fortunes, philosophies regarding individualism, and... one of us is a renowned author. The coincidence of discovery and timing became enchanting as Kate Chopin's life and words sent me a mystic whisper of connection that bridged more than 125 years.

Grandad Douglas Aleshire was a conductor on the 1855 train. His survival-without-a-scratch was akin to being a living crewman from the RMS Titanic. The train's plunge had its parallels to the ocean liner's maiden voyage. Eleven railcars were loaded with 600 dignitaries including the founder of St. Louis and the city's mayor, as well as bankers, judges, state legislators, their friends and children. The notables had been invited to the State Capital, Jefferson City, to celebrate the kick-off of what was to be the Pacific Railroad's, and State of Missouri's bid to become the gateway to Manifest Destiny by connecting the east and west coasts of the USA.

The construction of the trestle was incomplete on November 1, 1855, and girded with temporary supports. Torrential rains persisted throughout the day and political egos overruled caution. As the train chugged toward Jefferson City, it reached the trestle that was a half mile south of the confluence of the muddy Missouri River and the mucky Gasconade. The bridge succumbed to the weight of the locomotive, railcars, and dignitaries. Rescuers discovered forty-three passengers had been killed, and hundreds more were injured. A surviving junior editor of *The Western Journal* business magazine would recount the occurrence:

"In transport and solitude, I was sitting in a small saloon, over the last wheels of the last car, gazing out of the back window... when, seven miles west of Hermann, at nearly half past one o'clock, gradually and quietly, the car stopped and all was still. Thinking that Mr. O'Sullivan (the engineer) had stopped the cars to give passengers a view of the bridge, I arose from the window.... the pleasing charm by which I had been spell-bound was broken. An awful abyss opened wide before me. I stood on its brink. Only one— the last— car remained on the track. Ten laid in ruins. One car was hanging on the abutment.... A man was hanging by his arm through the window of the car. I caught him by the collar of his coat, and as he struggled with his hands and feet, drew him safely through the window of the car to the firm rocks of the precipice... All of the other passengers had sunk down into the front part below; and the groans of the wounded and dying ascended from the chasm, as from an infernal region, while the wind was howling, and the rain beating down in torrents."

The *Missouri Republican* newspaper of November 2, 1855, published a combined article of the inaugural trip and the ensuing tragedy; it ends with words that may as well have been written by Kate Chopin (then five-year-old Katherine O'Flaherty), "How little do we know what an hour may bring forth."

There was no table to turn the train at Jeff City, so another locomotive was behind the last car travelling backwards. It was supposed to hook up with the cars in Jeff City once the backslapping celebration had ended and parting gifts were imparted – then pull the cars back to St. Louis. It hauled wounded survivors instead.

Along the way back, an astute engineer wondered about a similar crossing at Boeuf Creek that had been successfully crossed earlier in the day. Reinspection revealed that it too was sinking. The beleaguered Pacific Railroad was halted like Napoléon at Waterloo. Walking injured crossed the bridge on foot while others were ferried in jon boats to await river steamers and another rescue train. Lord only knows how many died in the wait, and if Kate's father was one.

St. Louis was the lynchpin of American expansion in 1855. The Gateway City closed for several hours of funerals one day that year; one of the hours was for Thomas O'Flaherty. My great-great grandfather was there, along with five-year-old Kate, and her mother. Later, they all watched the railroad get ravaged by corruption, then Civil War. They didn't mourn when the nation's transportation hub departed St. Louis for Chicago, the loss was more subtle than a train wreck.

Douglas Aleshire, of Illinois, left the railroad and went on to establish an insurance company that would thrive then be sold to a conglomerate. The story of an hour brought deeper context to how my mother's family became once-wealthy after a man who narrowly escaped death built an organization to serve families of those who don't. How could I not ruminate on the uneven parallels of the O'Flaherty and Aleshire families... of me and Kate? What goes around comes around, then goes and comes around again.

In my Googling, I saw images of Katherine O'Flaherty Chopin. It was no surprise that she looked like a composite of women from western Illinois and east Missouri of the 19th and early 20th centuries. Stoic and stern and soft like the women who raised me; wise and witty, with a hint of loneliness that they would deny if asked.

I wouldn't have driven ten hours from our home in Minnesota to see the Gasconade site but, as further coincidence would have it, my wife is from the same Jeff City that invited wealthy St. Louisans across two suspicious bridges to a political extravaganza.

Central Missouri was balmy in December of 2021, requiring only short sleeves and a light jacket, so my brother-in-law liked the idea of a road trip to Gasconade to fill an empty slot on a day in a holiday week. We stopped at a country tavern, but not near the site. There's no saloon in Gasconade, no small-town café, not even a Casey's Quik Mart.

The village is nestled in a scenic valley at the confluence of the Missouri and Gasconade rivers, and even though it is home to two notable historic occurrences and a single whistle-stop from the high-traffic wineries of Hermann, Missouri, there has been no attempt to drive even the most modest tourist trade. The only signs of life in the little town of Gasconade double as signs of death.

The Pacific Railroad went down at Gasconade; Lewis & Clark camped and cut their surveying teeth there, then left.

When my brother-in-law and I went to the town with no place to wet a whistle, we went with hopes for discovery – with hopes of finding a link that brings a 166-year-old coincidence to life. Instead, we found neglected structures. An off-limits fence surrounded an Army Corps of Engineers base with a 40-acre campus of crumbling, century-old buildings that have been replaced by a tin shed and one soldier with an iPad. We found a small, six-by-nine-inch Lewis & Clark campsite marker with a .22 caliber dent.

In Gasconade, there's a ten-year-old rail trestle that is surely stout enough to support a trainload of dignitaries, but there's no sign of, or sign commemorating the Titanic-like plunge of 1855 railcars; not a murmur of coincidence that I could offer in condolence to Kate Chopin and her mother, not a high sign of hallelujah for my great-great grandfather who survived. There's no saloon or café, no plaque. Nothing but nothing. What really was missing was a sign that should read, "I'd turn back if I were you."

I was disappointed the folks of Gasconade didn't build a monument to the event that sent me a mystic whisper that bridged the ages, but realized it wasn't the locals who met Kate in a coincidence, so I had to move on to being thankful – and I was. I had discovered a new voice from 1894 and met a great author whom I've known all my life in the women who raised me.

In a couple days of reading, I watched Katherine O'Flaherty Chopin's life unfold, and relived my own family history. I read about life and corruption and death and courage. I saw a voice of sincere integrity get cancelled – then rightfully re-emerge.

I discovered in a coincidence that *The Story of an Hour...* is the story of life.

PART THIRTY-SEVEN

TILT THE PRISM

Seventy-two-point-seven years.

According to "the data," that's how long we can expect to live on this earth. In this New Age, we're becoming ever-more dependent on data from our scientists. It's the same in my old trade, marketing, where long ago the 'numbers game' replaced a good idea, a firm handshake, and hope.

Scientists, and baseball fans, have always been fanatical about statistics. The scientists have to be; we use their numbers to make life easier and more efficient, and as the chauffeur of our insatiable drive toward knowledge and greater truth. Philosophers, however, see numbers from a different angle. They tilt the prism to apply the variable of human experience, then watch the light go in a different direction.

Most of us have a Cliff Clavin friend or relative who has shared the Chinese proverb "Maybe so, maybe not," about a farmer's life of approximately 72.7 years.

In the proverb, the farmer's horse runs away, and his neighbors say, "Bad luck."

The farmer says, "Maybe so, maybe not."

The horse returns with several wild mares to breed and the neighbors say, "Great luck!"

Followed by, "Maybe so, maybe not."

The farmer's kid breaks his leg training a horse, and the "maybe so, maybe not" cycle repeats itself in a pattern as endless as the proverb's fundamental truth.

We're surrounded by truths that data says cannot exist — and truth is what makes life worth living.

Data tells us that in 1980, the Soviet hockey team had not lost a game in 12 years, that they defeated the United States 10-3 on February 9th, and would crush the U.S.A. again in the Olympics two weeks later. Then, the Americans tilted the prism toward a miracle.

According to the data, a fat, 3-legged dachshund named Ringo cannot beat six younger, healthier animals in a Weiner Dog Drag Race on a horse track, but I watched it happen, and won three bucks in the process.

At some point, our new discoveries meet Christopher Booker's *Seven Basic Plots*, and Mark Twain's assertion that there are no new ideas, merely old pieces of glass looked at through a new kaleidoscope. If Booker and Twain are right, we must ask ourselves if transitions between ages are really transitions, or are they simply cycles of data that have been forever blowing in the wind and churning in a can.

We know nasty little organisms that kill humans aren't new. Scientists have traced them back thousands of years and documented hundreds of epidemics — scores of which were far worse than the most recent. The bacteria known as "The Plague" visited the planet for hundreds of years. From 1350 to 1665, it revisited London in a 20-year cycle to take 20 percent of the women, children, and men without discretion. The Cocolitzli virus mysteriously killed up to 80 percent of Mexico's indigenous population in the 1500s. The Spanish Flu of 1918 took 50 million souls from the globe. Smallpox, Cholera, Yellow Fever… it goes on and on.

Our souls are no more sacred than those of the past, yet each Age of humans views themselves with the Arrogance of Infinity – we're more sophisticated, more "woke" than ever. Our modern sophistications cease, however, when we get the 'Past Due' notice from Mother Nature telling us all debts – public, private, or otherwise – are payable on demand without further notice.

The fine print of the notice may as well have been printed on Gutenberg's first press. It always reminds us of our collective vulnerability, and that our only defense as a species is natural immunity to the organisms that seek to consume and destroy us.

Scientists like to research and debate whether humanity has hit a hard limit in its evolution. I don't know what the debate is about. We've seen the same types of cataclysms and the same human reaction a million times since we learned how to write and set type. As Mr. Booker has accurately observed and noted, we *Overcome the Monster,* then experience *Comedy, Tragedy, and Rebirth.*

We have a recurring habit of slipping into false senses of security, and do so with everything precious: love, freedom, riches… our habits lead the wise to write timeless parables, proverbs, and moral fables to warn ourselves about ourselves.

Odds are, in addition to life's basic challenges, each of us will experience 3.3 world-class calamities in our 72.7 years. After battling the oppressor, dodging the bombs, or isolating and washing our hands, we're left to Booker's 'Rebirth' – to pick up the old pieces of glass and rebuild the kaleidoscope despite incredible pain and hardship.

Fate sweeps its path with no equity, no justice, no credit review.

FDR's "Nothing to fear but fear itself" speech has become a cliché in the 21st century, but it's as true as ever. Americans aren't afraid of hard work and great challenge – we relish that. We're laden with material obsession and afraid of some unknown force that might take our possessions. We're afraid of having an old car, if our clothes aren't chic, or our hair isn't done just so. We're afraid of what others, and the data, might say about us.

We fear past due notices before they arrive. We lament the ways we could have prepared but didn't. We live like the Lion and Mouse, the Ant and Grasshopper, the Tortoise, the Wolf, the Three Little Piggies, and the choker of the Golden Goose. When disasters occur, the pointed fingers of blame come out; the gerrymanderers and political dividers who had slithered into hiding return - with old glass in a new can.

There are no new stories. Life is a cyclical experience viewed through a rotating lens.

In our reflective moments – when we tilt the prism to see the data in a new light – we can clearly see that unity builds during times of shared sacrifice. We look harder for truth. We turn to parables, humor, and to thoughtful kindness more often. We pause in thanks, and hope, and wonder if we've hit a pivotal point in our lives, and our collective history.

The answer is always the same: "Maybe so, maybe not... maybe not."